Who's Afraid of Solarin?

Who's Afraid of Solarin?

*(Includes the first Tai Solarin Memorial Lecture, **'The Individual and the Challenges of Commitment in an Anomic Society,'** given to the Tai Solarin Organization in 2004)*

Femi Osofisan

University Press PLC
IBADAN ABA ABUJA AJEGUNLE AKURE BENIN IKEJA ILORIN
JOS KANO MAKURDI ONITSHA OWERRI WARRI ZARIA

©Femi Osofisan 2007
First published in 1978

ISBN 978 978 069 1714

Printed by Polygraphics Ventures Limited, Ibadan
Published by University Press PLC
Three Crowns Building, Jericho, P.M.B. 5095, Ibadan, Nigeria
Fax: 02-2412056 E-mail: unipress@universitypressplc.com
Website: www.universitypressplc.com

To the memory of **Dr Tai Solarin**
*former Principal and Proprietor
Mayflower Grammar School, Ikenne
& one-time Public Complaints Commissioner
of the old Western State of Nigeria
and
with his permission
also to*
Jide Malomo
wherever he may be with the ancestors

CAST

Chief James Dada Gbonmiaiyelobiojo (popularly known as 'JDG'): *Chairman of the Local Government Council*
Tolu: *his wife*
Mr Ayokanmi Olaitan: *Chief Magistrate*
Dr Bodunrin Alade-Martins: *Chief Medical Officer*
Chief Funso Fowolu (*aka* 'Force-is-Force', or 'F.F'): *Councillor for Education and Works*
Mrs Abeni Mailo: *Price Control Officer*
Miss Kaokudi Animasaun: *Councillor for Cooperatives and Agriculture*
Polycap: *Houseboy to JDG*
Baba Fawomi: *Ifa Priest*
Lamidi *and* **Lemomu:** *professional beggars*
Pastor Nebuchadnezzar Ifagbemi
Cecilia: *his daughter*
Isola Oriebora: *a traveller from Lagos*

PART ONE

(Morning. Sitting room of Chief Gbonmiaiyelobiojo, gaudily decorated).

*To one side, the Chief Magistrate Mr Ayokanmi Olaitan is playing **ayo** with the Price Control Officer, Mrs Abeni Mailo, while the medical doctor, Bodunrin Alade-Martins, stands by watching, smoking a pipe. Mrs Mailo, apparently affected by the tobacco smell, has one corner of her wrapper to her nose.*

To the other side, the Councillor for Education and Works, Chief Funso Fowolu, is having some dispute over a large sheaf of papers with the Councillor for Cooperatives, Miss Kaokudi Animashaun.

Polycap, the tired houseboy, is asleep in one corner on the floor, and would have been unnoticed but for his regular powerful snores.

Madam Gbonmiaiyelobiojo crosses over to the Chief Magistrate with some bottles).

CHIEF MAGISTRATE: *(Hardly controlling his irritation).* No, Madam, I shall not be buying perfume! *(Turning to his game).* Play! *(Hissing).* The idea!
PRICE CONTROL OFFICER: *(Hastily).* Same for me, Madam. Thank you.
(The Doctor has turned his back, coughing, to avoid her. Madam Gbonmiaiyelobiojo leaves the room, through the front door leading to her boutique, at the same time as her husband enters.)

CHAIRMAN: (*Waving aside the greetings from the Councillors*). It's not a good morning, as you will soon find out, my dear fellows. I hope my wife has not been bothering you. She's a bit, er - (*Gestures to his head*). Now to business. Have you heard the news?

COUNCILLOR FOR COOPERATIVES: Yes, they say they're taking away our car allowance. It's a disgrace. It was all in the news this morning.

COUNCILLOR FOR EDUCATION: And I say we should call a Press Conference immediately. Imagine the cheek of it all. They didn't even have the manners to inform us first before blaring it on the radio.

COUNCILLOR FOR COOPERATIVES: That's not the point of our complaint, you eunuch. After all, your appointment as a Director of the National Breweries came to you first on the radio. You didn't reject it.

COUNCILLOR FOR EDUCATION: Don't be silly! Is it the same thing? Why are you women always confusing issues? Or you know how much I paid for that appointment? And who's a eunuch if—

CHAIRMAN: (*Cutting in*). What are you two *jabbering* about? Must you take everything as an excuse for your endless *wrangulations*? I tell you the whole sky's about to tear apart on our heads, and you begin these inane arguments!

COUNCILLOR FOR COOPERATIVES: It's the man you went and put in charge of Education. God pity our children. They call him 'Force is Force', and he has to prove his nickname by bullying a lady.

COUNCILLOR FOR EDUCATION: Lady! Look at this unnamed monster, who eats up Council contracts like a woodworm. She calls herself a lady, and every layer of fa⸱ on her is the loot from some local Cooperatives!

COUNCILLOR FOR COOPERATIVES: And what of you? Is it the burden of plunder from the UPE[1] buildings project that keeps you stunted?

CHAIRMAN: Will you listen to me!

CHIEF MAGISTRATE: (*To Mrs Mailo, who has been watching the quarrel*). Play! In my court, I never permit prevarication!

PRICE CONTROL OFFICER: It's your turn. Ask Doki, if he can release his mouth long enough to talk. Stinking chimney!

CHAIRMAN: Gentlemen – and ladies – I said, have you heard the news?

CHIEF MAGISTRATE: It can't be my turn. And I'm never wrong, in my court. Impossible! In fact I remember playing—

COUNCILLOR FOR EDUCATION: All because I refuse to let you encroach on the school lands for your poultry scheme—

COUNCILLOR FOR COOPERATIVES: You can't stop me, let me tell you! The OFN[2] has priority over any other project, school or no school—

COUNCILLOR FOR EDUCATION: Oh yes, I know. Especially as the farm's to be established in your name.

CHIEF MAGISTRATE: God, how can a man concentrate? In my court, I ask the clerk—

---

[1] UPE: Universal Primary Education, a pet project, under various names, of most African governments.

[2] OFN: 'Operation Feed the Nation', another government pet programme, designed to encourage general public participation in agriculture.

COUNCILLOR FOR COOPERATIVES: I have told you again and again. You can come into it if you want. I have left you the first choice of over thirty percent of the remaining shares.

COUNCILLOR FOR EDUCATION: Who wants that ant's morsel? You can keep it. I remember offering you forty-five percent of the shares of Morise Construction Company when we were going to rehabilitate the Council roads. Fifty-five percent, free of charge!

DOCTOR: Listen to that! (*Coughs*). Both of you share everything and it still isn't enough. All we do at these meetings is— (*Breaks off coughing*)— excuse me, all we do is just rubberstamp your insatiable grabbing! (*Coughs*).

CHAIRMAN: (*Quite beside himself*). Gentlemen— (*He is interrupted by Polycap's heavy snoring*). For Christ's sake! (*Kicks Polycap awake*). Is this your bedroom, idiot! I can't hear myself think because of your snoring!

POLYCAP: (*Only half-awake*). I sorry too much sah. I go put am for number two gear—(*Tries to go back sleep*).

CHAIRMAN: (*Kicking him harder*). What *cheeks*! Get up at once! And run to Baba Fawomi, and—(*Shouting*) where do you think you're going?

POLYCAP: (*Pausing at the door, quite surprised*). To Baba Fawomi, as you tell me sah.

CHAIRMAN: And you won't wait for the message? Oh my head! Go and tell Baba Fawomi that I want him here at once. He's to drop everything he's doing, even if he has the Governor with him, and hurry here immediately. Tell him, it's an emergency.

(Polycap disappears. The room has come to a deathly stillness).

CHIEF MAGISTRATE: Baba Fawomi! In my court, I swear that— What, JDG, did I hear you right?

CHAIRMAN: Perhaps now you'll listen to me. I said— *(Shouting across to his wife, who is entering at that moment with some goods)*— Sorry, Tolu, you can't come in now. We're busy. *(She stretches out her arms, showing jewellery).* No! Nobody wants to buy jewellery! Not now! *(Shuts the door in her face. Returns, calming himself with great difficulty).* Okay, Okay, Gbonmiaiyelobiojo, remember, don't call her names. Not before visitors. *(Calms down).* I'm sorry, ladies and gentlemen, you all know how it is when a woman opens a new boutique. As I was saying—

PRICE CONTROL OFFICER: As I was going to say, JDG! As I was about to say! What's all this about Baba Fawomi? Let me remind you that I, Abeni, second daughter of the late renowned organist and lay preacher, Reverend Durosimi, I am a staunch Christian. I belong to the ranks of the First Pentecostal Movement of the Lagos Bar Beach. My Bible, bought in London, was blessed ten years ago by no less a personality than the General Overseer Ezekiah Ijonru himself, at a ceremony from which you departed, if I remember right, wobbling on your feet with drink. And that's not all, if his eminence *(Indicating the Doctor)* will stop belching smoke in my face. I have a rosary from a special curio shop in Jerusalem, birthplace of the Saviour. (*Courtesies piously*).I pay my dues also every Sunday to the First CMS Cathedral. If he thinks he can intimidate me— (*As Doki tries to stop her*)—No, I have not finished! If he thinks he can intimidate me, Abeni Mailo, daughter of Rev. Durosimi, by bringing in juju here, he's wasting his time!

CHAIRMAN: Have you finished, Madam? For Christ's sake I'm trying to tell you we're all in a terrible mess, (*He pronounces it 'mens'*) but you won't listen. Will your Bible, bought in Jerusalem—

PRICE CONTROL OFFICER: London, JDG! Oxford Street.

CHAIRMAN: Confound it! No, no, don't *loosen* your temper, Gbonmiaiyelobiojo...I'm sorry, but...(*Shouts*) I don't give a damn where your Bible was bought, Abeni! Do you think it can save you from the Public Complaints Commissioner? (*Gasps all around*).

CHIEF MAGISTRATE: (*Recovering slowly*). Did you say...the Public Complaints Commissioner? In my court, I—

DOCTOR: It's a joke, isn't it? Ha, ha, I see you're using your old election tactics again! (*Breaks into a fit of coughing*). Very funny!

CHAIRMAN: It's not a joke! I have information from...er, very reliable sources, that he's coming here. If he's not here already.

CHIEF MAGISTRATE: Solarin?

CHAIRMAN: I don't know for sure. But someone has been sent from headquarters, and he's travelling incognito.

CHIEF MAGISTRATE: Incognito! *Soponna*[3] o! It must be Solarin.
CHAIRMAN: What's worse, he has *secret* instructions.
CHIEF MAGISTRATE: It's Solarin! We're doomed. I don't think I can continue this game. I'm feeling sick.
COUNCILLOR FOR EDUCATION: I, I'm on leave, right from this moment! If anyone asks for me, I can't be found.
COUNCILLOR FOR COOPERATIVES: And I too. I'm going for treatment — in Cairo!
COUNCILLOR FOR EDUCATION: Why Cairo?
COUNCILLOR FOR COOPERATIVES: The address is in Arabic, who here can read it? And I'm leaving right away. (*They try to run out*).
CHAIRMAN: Stop there, both of you! (*Whips out a cutlass*). I forgot to mention it, but no one's going to move one *pinch* from this place until Baba Fawomi comes.
CHIEF MAGISTRATE: But ... why ...?
CHAIRMAN: We have an oath to take.
COUNCILLOR FOR COOPERATIVES: An oath!
CHAIRMAN: This is a serious matter and we must treat it *emergently*. I mean, I trust everybody here, but, still, one must forestall human weaknesses. If one of us, at a weak moment, yields to temptation, and rinses his mouth off before the Commissioner, think of the damage that would occur. I mean, I'm not thinking of myself. But the good reputation of our town, which I swore to defend, when I took office...
CHIEF MAGISTRATE: I'm on your side, JDG. Let's all swear. In my court, I place their hands on the Bible or the

---

[3] *Soponna* is the dreaded Yoruba god of small-pox.

Koran and then I whisper quietly to them that there's piece of iron in the book. You can't imagine what wonderful results I get. The truth is mercifully withheld, and the client freed.

DOCTOR: But this Commissioner - Oh my God, *secret* instructions!

COUNCILLOR FOR COOPERATIVES: It's outrageous. It's utterly heartless. What have we done?

COUNCILLOR FOR EDUCATION: I suspected something terrible would happen today, but I thought it was merely seeing your face. All night long I had this terrifying dream about a giant rat.

COUNCILLOR FOR COOPERATIVES: There you are. You simply have no heart at all, do you? Who asked you to go and dream up such a calamity? Couldn't you find any other animals than rats? And did it have to be a giant one?

CHAIRMAN: Gentlemen—and ladies—I want—

CHIEF MAGISTRATE: There must be a hidden motive in all this. I spy the hand of God. Ah, in my court—

COUNCILLOR FOR EDUCATION: It's as plain as daylight if you ask me. We begged you, didn't we, not to throw that poor man in jail last week. But you said you wanted his wife—

CHIEF MAGISTRATE: Nonsense! All members of the judiciary are entitled to the benefits of the profession. In my court, we do not shy away from our responsibilities. And you're a good one to talk. What happened to all the money sent from Lagos for the UNESCO classrooms project? For all we know, that's why the Commissioner is coming here.

COUNCILLOR FOR EDUCATION: How mean can you get? You know very well that the plans of those school buildings are all ready in my office. You saw the beautiful designs, the pride of any artist in the world.

COUNCILLOR FOR COOPERATIVES: So it's inside the plans that the children will learn to read and write? School's supposed to be starting next week.

COUNCILLOR FOR EDUCATION: So what! Rome was not built in a day. Go and bring your Commissioner here to catch me, since I see that this is all a conspiracy. Just remember Mandela! Many eminent men have gone to prison before and have come out only to become Heads of State. So bring your Commissioner, but make sure that when he's here he doesn't take a look also at OFN accounts.

CHAIRMAN: I knew it! I knew you were coming round to me. I knew you would end it all on my head.

COUNCILLOR FOR COOPERATIVES: I don't mean you, JDG. It's Kaokudi, this corrupt Council off—

CHAIRMAN: What's the difference! You think the Complaints Commissioner is going to remember that? You think that— (*Shouts at his wife, as she enters*) No, Tolu, no one's buying any lipstick here! No, nor wigs either! Please, go! (*Pushes her out*). Oh my head! Control, control, Gbonmialaiyelobiojo... As I was saying, the Public Complaints Commissioner knows I am the Chairman of the Council, and all responsibility for *expendition* will naturally fall on me. Even including the funds for the UNESCO project which you alone are hoarding at the moment so greedily, as if other people are not in need—

CHIEF MAGISTRATE: I said, in my court—
PRICE CONTROL OFFICER: But let us come to essentials, my dear colleagues. Stop all the clowning. As far as I can see, this is a subtle political move. Study it well, and you find all the ingredients. Yes, sirs! We're at a significant historical moment. For it means, my dear colleagues, that — er, let me see— that pipe, Doki, will ruin your life, let me tell you— yes, it means that we're about to be attacked!
DOCTOR: (*Coughing*). Attacked!
PRICE CONTROL OFFICER: By Britain, or America, though my guess is both. The enemies of Africa are about to pounce, spurred on by their imperialist ambitions. War's at our doorstep!
CHAIRMAN: But... but what's that got to do with us?
PRICE CONTROL OFFICER: What do you mean, Chief Gbonmiayelobiojo? The nation is in danger and you think the military boys, who have had experience of war all over the continent, are going to sit back and just fold their arms? No, sir, that's not how it happens in Political Science! Ask anyone in the Faculty. They'll tell you about me before I withdrew from the University—with the Senate's advice. I know all the tactics, down to the little tricks and subterfuges... The military boys, God bless them for their eternal vigilance, are sending a security agent here to sniff out disloyalty!
CHAIRMAN: What a brain! Oh my head's cracking! Mrs Abeni Mailo, my dear—oh, my head—we're not in any *stratategical* position here as far as the nation's security is concerned. We don't even have a military camp in the town!

PRICE CONTROL OFFICER: (*Confidentially*). You see!...
CHAIRMAN: (*Shouting*). No, I don't see! What's—
PRICE CONTROL OFFICER: Politics, Chief Gbonmiaiyelobiojo! International politics! Not like your ten naira local elections where you distribute bread and *moin-moin*[4] to entice the electorate. But the real thing, like pepper-soup! You like it or you don't like it, your eyes will still water! Ah, those of us who grew up in Lagos, and also honoured the campus of a University with our presence, we are familiar with all the details of international intrigue. Yes, what experience we had in those days when Awolowo and Azikiwe were fighting! In a flash Zik has taken control of Tinubu and begins to launch his missiles. And there is Awo in Campos Square, dodging here and there, and then here and there again, as they fall in a torrent all about him. And Zik is unrelenting: 'Serendipism!'... 'Democraticism!'... 'Scholasticism!'... 'Absolutism!'... 'Transitionalism!'... 'For Zikism is no Jingoism!'... Ah, Oga Zik, small, small! Don't kill the man! Until Awo, the great Awo, leader of the Yorubas, profiting from a moment of carelessness—great strategist, my friends!—suddenly raises his head and begins to repel the attack with his hidden anti-missile missiles! Wait, what is that? Ah, look at them my friends, how they dominate the air, Awo's stock of nuclear submarines... oh what a counter-attack! Zik of Africa, where are you now! Oh yes, for suddenly... er, what were we saying?

---

[4] Moin-moin: local bean pudding.

CHAIRMAN: If you can please come down from my chair, Abeni? (*She gets down*). Thank you. Ah, the number of idiots representing the people!

CHIEF MAGISTRATE: JDG, unless someone else has a speech to make, I think we must now decide, quickly. In my court, the practice is to retire for tea in the inner chambers and reflect. But in the absence of tea, even though an entertainment allowance was duly voted for the office of Council Chairman, well, I rule that we continue the hearing. What are we to do about this impending visit?

CHAIRMAN: I have called you here this morning to warn you. We must act fast to put our house in *under*. A war long predicted doesn't kill even the cripple, says the proverb. As soon as we finish with the oath, we must get to work. All relevant files must be sorted out, well dusted, and immediately disposed off!

COUNCILLOR FOR COOPERATIVES: How?

CHAIRMAN: Eat them, Madam! (*Tolu enters*) No, Tolu, please— oh, I must not rebuke her, not in the presence of strangers— Tolu, go away, no one here is interested in buying milk, this isn't a market! GET OUT!!! (*Pushes her out*). Oh Gbonmiaiyelobiojo, control yourself... ah, where was I? Please, a little forbearance, my dear colleagues, my wife is a bit, er— (*Gestures to his head*)...ah, yes, you Force is Force. The files on the UPE contracts must be burnt this very morning.

COUNCILLOR FOR EDUCATION: It can't be done. The whole office's in a mess. It will take ages to find the right files for eating— er, I mean, burning.

CHAIRMAN: God, what a brain! They're all bent on wrecking me. Can't you set the entire office on fire! It's your whole future that's in *jeopandry*, man, and would you rather save the office! And that reminds me. I know no man is free of sin— God made us that way, and I suppose He must have a purpose—but, starting from today, no one is to accept bribes again.

CHIEF MAGISTRATE: And gifts?

CHAIRMAN: And gifts! Is that clear?

CHIEF MAGISTRATE: It's going to be hard. In my court—

CHAIRMAN: You'll have to try, Ayo. But no one is to take any bribes at all except with specific clearance from me.

DOCTOR: (*Coughing*). I still don't understand why they've decided upon us. I suspect a vicious kind of ... of ... (*Coughing*) ... of witch-hunting! I mean, Ijebu-ode is nearer to them. So is Ondo, not to talk of Oyo! Even Akure is still closer to them. (*Coughs*). And all those towns are much bigger than ours, with larger hospitals, far more customers—I mean patients—in one week that we see in a month. I know my colleagues in those places are raking quite a fortune and I am not complaining. But why not them, then? Why me?

COUNCILLOR FOR EDUCATION: Why us?

CHIEF MAGISTRATE: It's the heavy hand of God.

CHAIRMAN: Maybe so, maybe so. Doki, since you mention it, I'm sure the hospital will be one of the first places the Commissioner will want to see, and—

DOCTOR: Are you acc— (*Coughing*)— accusing me, JDG?

CHAIRMAN: God, there's no time for that! I—
DOCTOR: (*Coughing badly*) Because ... because I can ... tell you I do my work... just as conscientiously as... any other person here. It isn't my fault the place is ... horribly congested. Excuse me. What can ... you do with a Catering De... de ...de... department, excuse me, which, in spite of all our warnings, insists... insists, excuse me, on providing such arresting odours that the patients, instead of recovering and leaving for ... for their homes, excuse me, very often prefer to stay and end their lives in our wards? Tell me! (*Another round of coughing. Abeni puts her arms round his shoulder. He shrugs her off rather brusquely. Her disappointment is very apparent*). I see to it ... myself... that, that... excuse me, that there are never enough beds to accommodate them, but—
CHAIRMAN: No one's accusing you, Bodunrin. We all have our little *frailings*. All I'm saying is that you should get the place cleaned up as fast as possible. And the patients, get them to have their bath, at least once a week! And also put on some decent nightgowns...
DOCTOR: Night-gown! Why don't you recommend a beaded crown for each of them. (*Coughs*).
CHAIRMAN: All right, all right, do your best. As for the mortuary, which is even more congested—Well, at least get rid of all the corpses on the floor, or lock the place up for some time. Oh dear, oh dear! Ah Gbonmiaiyelobiojo, uneasy lies the head! (*Turning to the Chief Magistrate*). Ayo, as for

you, I think you ought to spend more time in the court, if only as a hobby. I went there yesterday and, do you know, the place is *lettered* with fowls!

CHIEF MAGISTRATE: Yes, I know. In my court, even the attendants take OFN seriously. Why, we have to charge a bit more on the oaths and affidavits to maintain the poultry. I'm sure the Commissioner'll be impressed.

CHAIRMAN: It's misplaced zeal, I tell you. ... oh my head...

CHIEF MAGISTRATE: Very well then. I shall order the attendants to take the fowls over to my kitchen at once. Will you like to come for dinner tonight?

CHAIRMAN: Not tonight. I mean—(*Tolu enters*). Tolu, again! I am going to lose my temper! I am going to abuse you, you *aggrabevating* witch! I am going to— Get out! Is this the moment to sell pillow-case! (*Chases her out*). Ah Gbonmiaiyelobiojo, what devil pushed you into allowing her to open that shop?

CHIEF MAGISTRATE: It's the heavy hand of God.

CHAIRMAN: Then let it fall on you, that heavy hand of God!

BABA FAWOMI: (*Entering on the last sentence*). Edumare[5] never lays his hands amiss. For he's never against those who are willing to help themselves.

CHAIRMAN: (*Starting, like the others*). Baba Fawomi!

BABA FAWOMI: Sh, say nothing! As soon as I got your message, I consulted Ifa[6], and I am happy to inform you, my dear children, that Ifa has confirmed it, you have a problem.

---

[5] *Edumare*, or *Eledumare*, is the Yoruba word for God.
[6] *Ifa* is the Yoruba god of divination. The word is used also for the system of divinatin itself.

CHAIRMAN: We—

BABA FAWOMI: Hush, I say! I know everything. (*Winks*). Watch. (*He brings out his **opele**[7] and starts a mock ritual of divination, chanting words that are not recognizably Ifa's. Three times he throws the seeds and shakes his head, sighing heavily, and the three times, the Chairman and his men, who have crowded round the priest, collapse in terror and despair.*) That's the final proof! And I beg you, please don't mention the question of professional fees yet, for I shall only be too happy to accept.

COUNCILLOR FOR COOPERATIVES: One fat goat, Baba, from our best Government farm! To be delivered today at dusk.

COUNCILLOR FOR EDUCATION: Ten, no, fifteen per cent of the contract to be awarded next week for the proposed Cultural Centre!

DOCTOR: Free vaccination for you and your family against whatever disease is in vogue! (*Coughs*). And for future epidemics in the development plan.

CHIEF MAGISTRATE: One year's pardon in advance! For all crimes you may wish to commit, including murder! And the promise of a life term for all mischievous witnesses!

PRICE CONTROL OFFICER: First choice over any goods seized this month from hoarders! If only you can stop the public complaints Commissioner from coming here and—

BABA FAWOMI: (*Angrily*) I told you to be quiet! (*Throws seeds again with great solemnity*). Ifa accepts

---

[7] *Opele* is the name of the Ifa priest's divination tray.

the gifts. Professional fees will be settled later. (*Throws again*). Ha! It's serious, serious! Ifa says you are worried, my children. All of you without exception. And extremely worried too, because, as it appears, a certain visitor is coming!

DOCTOR: (*Eagerly*). Yes, yes! It's .... (*Stopped by cough*).

BABA FAWOMI: Quiet ! Will you give Ifa a chance or not? (*Packing his things*). Listen, Chief James-y, Doki, and others, if you'd rather do this yourself—

COUNCILLOR FOR EDUCATION: (*Clinging unto him*). No, please, Baba! Please help us.

BABA FAWOMI: Oh, you think it's as easy as that! You won't let Ifa tell you your problems and allow you to propose solutions. It's yap, yap, yap, all the time! It's outrageous! Outrageous! Ifa is supposed to see and talk clearly on a dry throat!

CHAIRMAN: My fault, Baba, please forgive me. Just give me one minute. (*Rushes to open the door. Polycap, who has been leaning on the door, eavesdropping, falls in*). Really!

(*The Chairman staggers back in fright, just as his guests, including Baba Fawomi who has rapidly collected his things in one desperate sweep, collide in their sudden rush for one of the windows*).

COUNCILLOR FOR EDUCATION: (*Screaming*). Save your lives, he's come! The Complaints Commissioner is here!

CHAIRMAN: (*Shaken, but recovering*). No, gentlemen. No. Ladies, please, it's only my house boy. (*As they return, shaken, to their places*). Polycap, explain yourself!

BABA FAWOMI: I've never seen a luckier devil. Ifa could have harmed you, you know. He was heading straight for you, I had to run to hold him back.

POLYCAP: No vex sah. Please tell Ifa say I sorry too much. Na fever dey do me sah.

CHAIRMAN: Fever!

POLYCAP: Yes, Master. The yellow one. Na my missis give me the infection, because I swear sah, yellow no be my favourite colour. But as God don join we assunder, nahim I go catch this yellow fever from my missis. Sometime sah I no know at all when I go dey wakka for sleep.

CHAIRMAN: (*Severely*). Polycap!

POLYCAP: Na true sah I swear! God bend our necks if I dey lie! The yellow fever, stupid bastard, nahim push me against the door—

CHAIRMAN: That's enough! Run quickly now and bring me a bottle of gin from under my bed. (*Polycap disappears*). Go on, Baba Fawomi, your drink's on the way. Let's hear the worst.

BABA FAWOMI: Sacrifice!

ALL: Pardon, Baba?

BABA FAWOMI: Sacrifice! That's the only way to redeem your sins. For Ifa says he has seen you all, and every one of you is a rogue. No, don't protest, look at the seeds yourself. Every act of your life is exposed in these patterns. (*Looking at them in turn*). The fornications, adulteries, forgeries, small and big embezzlements! The betrayals, the stupid suspicion of people trying to help you! Your miserliness, especially to priests! No, I won't go on, you all have enough crimes in your lives to justify your posts!...

CHAIRMAN: All right, Baba. Tell us how much it will cost us to repent.

BABA FAWOMI: You must sacrifice urgently. Ifa says categorically that unless you perform the appropriate sacrifices without delay, he that is awaited will soon be here!

COUNCILLOR FOR EDUCATION: Good God!

BABA FAWOMI: And the visitor coming is— yes, you're lucky, Ifa is eloquent today, everything is clear— the man coming is... the Public Complaints Commissioner! (*Gasps all around. The Doctor's cough renews with greater vigour, but Abeni is patting his back*). And to prove all this, you— (*Pointing*)—yes, you, Ayokanmi! Ifa says you are about to ask a question.

CHIEF MAGISTRATE: Me! But I have no—

BABA FAWOMI: Don't be afraid. Aren't you the one in white buba?

CHIEF MAGISTRATE: (*Examining himself*). Yes, yes, indeed. Just imagine that! I am wearing white buba!

BABA FAWOMI: And I suppose you're not the Chief Magistrate?

CHIEF MAGISTRATE: Ah, I deserved the promotion, sir, and I won't take any one disputing it. I have paid my dues regularly to the secret cult[8] since I was an apprentice lawyer.

BABA FAWOMI: You see. Ifa is never wrong. Is your first son not left-handed, through your aunt's witchcraft?

CHIEF MAGISTRATE: But... but I never had an aunt! And all my sons are right-handed, like me.

---

[8] Membership of secret cults has reportedly been the bane of the judiciary; so serious that the government once tried to stop it by legislation.

BABA FAWOMI: All? Think again. What of the one going to be born next year by—*(Shouting at him)*—THAT WOMAN WHOSE HUSBAND YOU'VE JUST THROWN IN JAIL!!!

CHIEF MAGISTRATE: *(Hastily).* Oh yes, yes, a slip of memory! I'll do anything you say, Baba Fawomi.

BABA FAWOMI: Just ask your question, and stop beating about the bush. Go on, He is listening.

(As he searches for what to say, the others shout at him, impatiently: "Will you just go ahead and ask your question, fool!", "Come on, idiot, don't waste our time!", etc.).

CHIEF MAGISTRATE: I'm ready to cooperate, I swear... but, Baba, could you just give me a hint about this question I'm going to ask?

(The others grow even more irritated.)

BABA FAWOMI: *(Relenting).* Look at the man! He's so forgetful! Well, I'll help you. Ayo, you were going to—

CHAIRMAN: *(As Tolu enters).* Confound it, Tolu! How many times must I warn you not to disturb us? Oh, Gbonmiayelobiojo, control yourself, especially in the presence of Ifa. Tolu, please, I'm begging you— *(But, unable to control himself, he shouts at her)* ...you're a none-skull! Your father is a zero-skull! Your mother is a minus-skull! And all of your wretched family are minus-minus-skulls! Get out! go and find other clients for your saucepans! *(She runs out)* Oh my head. I'm sorry, Baba Fawomi, for the interruption. It's my wife, she's a bit— *(Gestures to his head).* Please continue.

BABA FAWOMI: Ifa can cure it, later. Ayokanmi, you were going to ask me what sacrifices are needed.
CHIEF MAGISTRATE: Of course, that's it. I was indeed going to ask.
BABA FAWOMI: Ifa says, considering the gravity of the matter, you will each need five cows—
CHIEF MAGISTRATE: Easy enough, five cows.
BABA FAWOMI: Will you let me finish! Plus ten goats, of the home-grown type, all black and fat—
COUNCILLOR FOR COOPERATIVES: (*Groans*). Ten fat goats.
BABA FAWOMI: Ten other goats, of the brown variety—
DOCTOR: (*Coughing*). Ten other goats!
BABA FAWOMI: Of the brown variety. I'll continue. You also need sixteen fowls—
PRICE CONTROL OFFICER: Sixteen fowls!
BABA FAWOMI: Strong-limbed, home-raised chickens! Not these lifeless ones from the Government Farm which do not allow your teeth sufficient exercise.
CHAIRMAN: (*Groaning*). Is that all!
BABA FAWOMI: Yes, for the first part of the ceremony. The invocation. Then, for the ceremony proper, each of you will fetch seven bales of white cloth—
CHAIRMAN: Seven bales!
BABA FAWOMI: *Sanyan,* preferably, with attractive designs. And after that—
POLYCAP: (*Running in, panting*). Here's the bottle sah.
(*Again, the Commissioners who have scattered in fear, reassemble.*)
CHAIRMAN: Couldn't you knock before rushing in? And why are you panting?
POLYCAP: You tell me to run sah.

CHAIRMAN: But the bedroom is only two doors away.
POLYCAP: Yes, sah, if you take the shortest route.
CHAIRMAN: Oh my head! The boy's an absolute idiot!
BABA FAWOMI: Ifa forgives him and accepts the drink. (*Takes the bottle and drinks greedily. Suddenly he chokes violently and staggers up, clutching his throat*). Yeh! Ye-pah! I am dead! I have been assassinated! Tell my clients, I died bravely. They should not forget the debts they're owing! (*They run to him*).
DOCTOR: (*Coughing*). Give ... way! Give way!
COUNCILLOR FOR EDUCATION: What happened? JDG, what have you done?
BABA FAWOMI: (*Struggling bravely*). Poison! I am poisoned!
CHAIRMAN: (*Distraught*). Poison? Let me see the bottle. (*Takes it and exclaims*). Ah, Polycap! What have you done to me? Polycap, this is deicide! You have killed a god in my parlour!
POLYCAP: It's not possible, sah. God is immortal. The catechist said that—
CHAIRMAN: Damn the catechist! I don't care what he said! You've gone and given poison to Orunmila.
POLYCAP: Orunmila! But I've never even met the man sah. I swear to—
CHAIRMAN: Quiet! (*Thrusting bottle at him*). Look at the bottle you brought, what's on the label?
POLYCAP: (*After taking a long, sober look*). I can't see anything on it sah.
CHAIRMAN: Oh my head! Can't you read?
POLYCAP: No sah.
CHAIRMAN: I know you can't read, shut your mouth! Oh my head! They're all over the place! What are our

women eating to *spawn* imbeciles in such generous numbers? This, Polycap, is liquid soap for the toilet. The one you were wasting before I put it away.

POLYCAP: (*Whistling*) Tchei! But how he come enter the gin bottle sah? What a dirty trick!

CHAIRMAN: Get out! Get out! (*Polycap runs out, as Tolu enters*). No, not again! Help me! Gbonmiaiyelobiojo will run crazy. He will beat her! He will—oh, Ifa is present. Control it, please. Tolu, I'm *applying* to you, nobody here wants to buy a plastic doll. Okay? Go! (*Pushes her and slams door in her face*).

BABA FAWOMI: (*Who has packed his things*) Don't bother to shut the door, I am leaving. Giving toilet soap to Orunmila! You're going to sacrifice a lot to purge this. And as for the Public Complaints Commissioner, forger it, you're lost! I have already uttered a terrible curse to bring him here! He'll soon be arriving.

ALL: (*In consternation*). What, Baba Fawomi! You won't do that! Not to old clients? Consider our families! Think of the reputation of the town that will suffer! Think of the name of the fatherland!

BABA FAWOMI: Out of my way! Next you will be emptying your chamberpots in Ifa's mouth. Oh my throat!

ALL: (*Still restraining him*). Pity, Baba. Have pity. Revoke the curse!

BABA FAWOMI: Let me go, I say! You will see me in my house first before I agree to change my mind. And if you know what is good for you, you will come properly loaded. Goodbye. (*He goes out*).

COUNCILLOR FOR EDUCATION: Let's follow him quickly.

DOCTOR: But what—(*Coughing*)—laxatives does one prescribe for Ifa? Ehn?

COUNCILLOR FOR EDUCATION: JDG, see what you've done? I won't be surprised at all if the Commissioner knocks the door at this very minute and says—

(A sudden knock on the door. Everybody freezes. The knock is repeated. Petrified, they begin to retreat slowly against the wall).

LAMIDI: (*Putting his head in*). Is no one at—(*Sees the people cowering against the wall*). Oh I'm sorry, I didn't know you were rehearsing for the festival.

COUNCILLOR FOR EDUCATION: (*Bellowing, as he recovers*). What the hell are you doing here!!!

CHAIRMAN: (*Wiping his face*). Please, it's okay. He's a friend.

COUNCILLOR FOR COOPERATIVES: A friend, this beggar?

CHAIRMAN: It's okay, I assure you. It's my information service. Where's your partner? Come in, come in, I suppose you have news for me.

(Two men, dressed as beggars, come in).

DOCTOR: (*Coughing*). There are ... excuse me, two of them.

CHAIRMAN: Yes, they're professional beggars. There's nothing wrong with them. In fact they were clerks with the Council before they went into full-time practice. They gather information for me about rumour-mongers and *propential* trouble-makers in the town. Speak, introduce yourselves to my friends.

LAMIDI: (*Making an elaborate bow*). Lamidi, your Excellencies.

LEMOMU: (*Same act*). Lemomu. We know all about you, it's our business to.

CHIEF MAGISTRATE: Wait a minute. Were you not the ones I saw prowling around my car two nights ago?

LAMIDI: Your Excellency has a good memory. Lemomu saw you entering the woman's house and—

LEMOMU: —And, knowing her husband was away, resting in the 'White College'[9] by your consent, we—

CHIEF MAGISTRATE: (*Hastily*). All right, all right, you scoundrels. Just let me catch you near me again!

LAMIDI: No offence meant, sir. It was just in the line of business.

LEMOMU: And the news we bring will compensate.

CHAIRMAN: Go on. What news?

LAMIDI: Are you all right? Is everybody okay?

CHAIRMAN: Don't be an idiot. Speak!

LAMIDI: Well, get ready for a shock.

CHAIRMAN: Go ahead with it, for God's sake.

LAMIDI: Shall I tell it, Lemomu, or should I leave it to you?

LEMOMU: (*Graciously*). No, go ahead please.

LAMIDI: You won't mind?

LEMOMU: I assure you.

LAMIDI: You know it's your turn today.

LEMOMU: I waive my rights. I can't match your power of eloquence, you've always said it. And this is a very special treatment.

LAMIDI: So you want me to tell it?

LEMOMU: Why should I deceive you?

---

[9] A common euphemism for prison.

LAMIDI: The news is important. There may be a bonus.
LEMOMU: We'll share it. If you consent.
LAMIDI: We've always shared.
LEMOMU: Equally.
LAMIDI: When the clients are kind.
LEMOMU: Or when their palms are dry.
LAMIDI: All our assets.
LEMOMU: Our liabilities.
LAMIDI: Laila ilahla—
LEMOMU: Momodu yarah sulilah!

(They go into the familiar professional supplicatory chant used by beggars).

CHIEF MAGISTRATE: (*Scandalised*). JDG, what is this? In my court—
CHAIRMAN: It's all right, gentlemen—and ladies. I understand. (*Takes out money from his pocket, and gives beggars who cease the chant.*) Now talk!
LAMIDI: Thank you. But we know your honourable colleagues will not be left out of this show of generosity.
LEMOMU: They'll insist on following your example.
COUNCILLOR FOR COOPERATIVES: Does the news concern us?
LAMIDI: Very much, your Excellency.
LEMOMU: But not directly.
COUNCILLOR FOR EDUCATION: What do you mean?
LEMOMU: I mean, indirectly, your Excellency.
LAMIDI: It's about a certain visitor.
LEMOMU: Whom you are eagerly awaiting. (*The beggars chant*).

PRICE CONTROL OFFICER: (*Giving them money*). All right, you hounds, take. And it had better be good. (*The others follow suit, and the beggars stop their song.*)
LEMOMU: We thank you for remembering that beggars also have stomachs.
LAMIDI: Almost like yours.
LEMOMU: Which, alas, must eat.
LAMIDI: As yours also eat.
CHAIRMAN: Are we going to hear the news!!!
LAMIDI: Well, I'll tell it. It happened like this, your Excellencies. We woke up this morning, feeling terrible—
LEMOMU: *I* was feeling terrible. Lamidi, what's happened to your sense of detail? You were fine.
LAMIDI: Oh yes, Lemomu was feeling bad, and I—
CHAIRMAN: Damn it, to the point, Lemomu!—er, I mean Lamidi! Tell us what you *founded* out about the Public Complaints Commissioner!
LAMIDI: Well, if that's the way you want it. I am happy to inform you that he's already here. (*Gasps all around*)
COUNCILLOR FOR EDUCATION: Impossible!
CHAIRMAN: (*Incredulous*). What did you say, Lemomu?
LEMOMU: You mean, Lamidi.
CHAIRMAN: Yes, Lemomu! Lamidi! Oh confound it! Who is here?
LAMIDI: The man you're waiting for, the Complaints Commissioner.
PRICE CONTROL OFFICER: Is here already?
CHIEF MAGISTRATE: Solarin, is it?

LAMIDI: We didn't wait to be introduced.
CHAIRMAN: Oh God! Since when has he been here?
LEMOMU: Since Monday.
ALL: What!!!
LAMIDI: Only four days.
CHAIRMAN: Gentlemen, you heard that! The Commissioner's been here for four days!
COUNCILLOR FOR EDUCATION: We're lost. He's had time to find out everything.
CHAIRMAN: Wait. Tell me, how do you know this?
LEMOMU: By finding out, your Excellency.
CHAIRMAN: I know! I mean— oh my head! (*Tolu enters*). Tolu! I said... I said...oh Gbonmiaiyelobiojo, keep your temper, she's your wife. I said— (*Seizes cutlass and chases her out*). Get out! I'll chop your head! I'll spill blood! I'll get a divorce! (*Slams door and returns*). I'm sorry, friends, but you know how it is. She's a bit— (*Gestures to his head*). Who the hell wants to buy tomato puree in the present circumstances? I mean, the Commissioner is not for eating, that would be *cannibality*! Please tell us, where's he staying?
LAMIDI: With the pastor.
CHIEF MAGISTRATE: Impossible. The pastor's not a traitor. He can't afford it.
PRICE CONTROL OFFICER: He gets his weekly dues, but I should have suspected it—Smoke yourself right to hell, my dear, you think I care! The zeal with which the Pastor preaches about the devil should have put me on my guard. There was always some touch of admiration in it.

CHAIRMAN: My dear friends, we have no time to lose. The damage may still be checked. Go quickly to your offices and see what can still be retrieved through a *judicial* fire accident. I'll head straight for the Pastor's house with these two men.

LAMIDI: No thanks. We'd rather not come along.

LEMOMU: Professional etiquette, your Excellency.

LAMIDI: It would be betraying the Pastor to allow him to recognize us.

CHAIRMAN: But ... why!

LEMOMU: Charity is the only means his congregation can use to get to heaven.

LAMIDI: And what's the use of charity if there are no beggars to receive it? We're the Pastor's most reliable agents.

LEMOMU: When his members drop their coins—

LAMIDI: We're always there to receive! Good morning.
(The beggars go out chanting).

CHAIRMAN: Well, Ayo, how about you? Will you accompany me?

CHIEF MAGISTRATE: Not me. The court's supposed to be in session. The damned place hasn't even been swept for months. And those fowls! (*Goes out quickly*).

COUNCILLOR FOR EDUCATION: I'm going to have a few stalls destroyed immediately. Then we'll put up a board with the sign: NEW MARKET UNDER CONSTRUCTION. And I think I know which stalls to pull down.

(Goes. Muttering various excuses, the others also disappear).

CHAIRMAN:*(Running after them with cutlass)*. Polycap! Arrest them! *Manicure* one of them at least! Polycap! Stop them!

*(He runs out after them. **BLACKOUT.**)*

End of PART ONE.

PART TWO

(Almost the same time as at the end of the last scene. We are in the sitting-room of the PASTOR, Reverend Nebuchadnezzah Ifagbemi. It is more or less similar to the Chairman's in false opulence and gaudy taste, but it also combines a dining-room located at one end. Unlike the dark secretiveness of the Chairman's however, the windows here are wide open to let in a lot of light.
The Pastor, about the same age as the Chairman, is having an argument with his daughter, CECILIA).

PASTOR: I implore you Cecilia. Don't beg me. Even the charity of God has its limits.

CECILIA: But, father—

PASTOR: No! I know what you're going to say. I—

CECILIA: Sorry— *(She dusts off some speck of the furniture).*

PASTOR: Yes, God knows, I've always kept my house open even to the unfortunate. There are beggars in this town who, but for me, would long have been out of trade. That's why I took him in with all your insistence when he arrived and was in such a wretched condition. But I've been generous enough. He must go today.

CECILIA: Father—

PASTOR: Just think of it! Suppose your mother had been alive? Do you think she would approve his going about the house like this, behaving as if he owned it!

CECILIA: But you yourself told him to feel as free as if he were your own son. Sorry— *(Dusts off another speck).*

PASTOR: Well, I said so, but can't he understand proverbs? Is everything one says to be taken literally? Mustn't one think of propriety in everything?

CECILIA: All the same—

PASTOR: I know how much he must have hurt you by his brazen behaviour, poor child, even though you won't like to tell me. That's why I must be firm. The devil comes in too many rags and tears.

CECILIA: Father, I want—

PASTOR: Don't mention it, I understand. When he arrived—

CECILIA: Sorry— (*Dusts off another speck.*)

PASTOR: When he arrived, I took pity on him, at your bidding. No one can accuse me of having failed in my duty as the leading officer of Christ in this parish. I took care of him. Even against your objections, I personally made sure he gets the same food as the servants eat. And his room is one of the best, near the dog's kennel, where there's plenty of air—

CECILIA: Yes, foul air.

PASTOR: Exactly! And—I beg your pardon? What did you say?

CECILIA: I mean that, considering his status, father, he's been too kind to us.

PASTOR: What! He drank the remaining bottle of communion wine all by himself!

CECILIA: You see! What greater proof of his forbearance!

PASTOR: That's why—

CECILIA: Sorry— (*Dusts off another speck*).

PASTOR: That's why he couldn't leave any for your father? Is that a Christianly behaviour? And what's this you're saying about his status? What do you know about it?

CECILIA: I've been trying to tell you since yesterday, father. The man's an important official in Lagos, travelling about on some secret mission. He was attacked on Sunday night by armed robbers. That's how he arrived here on foot, his shirt in tatters. Sorry— (*Dusts off speck on Pastor's shirt*). And he's so handsome, father! I think it's a privilege to have him as our guest.

PASTOR: And I think not! I don't like his confiding the secrets of his life in you either. So what, if he was robbed by thieves, is that the kind of story a decent man should tell to ladies? It's armed seduction, I know his type. He'll have to leave today.

CECILIA: Father, no, you'll kill me!

PASTOR: I'll lend him the car—or, rather, no, I'll ask James. He's the Council Chairman, he should do something about it.

CECILIA: It would be so unfair to send him away like that. A man with such a sweet voice too.

PASTOR: I'll judge the sweetness when he's saying goodbye. What do you think I care about his voice, Cecilia! I'm surprised at you, you who have always been so level-headed. How do you know that all he told you isn't a mere pack of lies? If—

CECILIA: Sorry— (*Dusts off speck from furniture*).

PASTOR: I'd like to know why for instance he hasn't once stepped outside these premises since he came. He may be a wanted criminal for all we know.

CECILIA: But I told you, father. He's been convalescing. The robbers gave him a sound beating. Oh, if he hadn't fought back so gallantly. You should see the valiant stripes on his back. In various shades...

PASTOR: On his back! That decides it, he must leave at once. No decent official goes about disclosing the secrets on his back to an innocent girl, especially when her father's not present. Go and call him.

CECILIA: I assure you he did it decently, father. Don't you trust your own daughter to take after you? And he was so nice-looking with his shirt off. He looked just like that picture in your Bible.

PASTOR: Yes, the Devil, no doubt.

CECILIA: Father, you're blaspheming!

PASTOR: Call him out!

(ISOLA enters, very cheerful).

ISOLA: Please go on. I heard you talking about me, so I thought I'd come and contribute.

PASTOR: My dear sir, I...I...

CECILIA: Father, you won't dare! I'll never talk to you again!

PASTOR: Sir... shut up, Cecilia... Sir, you're ... wearing my shirt!

ISOLA: Yes. I didn't think you'd like me in your cassock.

PASTOR: My brand new shirt, sir!

ISOLA: I'll manage it. Ah, how quick you notice things. Excellent habit, Pastor, keep it up. (*Pumping his hand*). You know, I find we're just about the same size. Extra-ordinary. The ways of God are—what's the word again?

CECILIA: (*Eagerly*). Mysterious. Sorry— *(She helps to smoothen his collars)*.

ISOLA: Thank you, Cecilimisa-Misa.

PASTOR: What's that?

ISOLA: A term of endearment, Pastor. Not much known, I'm afraid, by you professionals in the bush. Ah, in Lagos! Along the fragrant Marina at night, with all the golden-yellow lights blinking like glow-worms! You should see the sea then, my friend, oh you should see the marvel, that enchanted moment, spread out like a bed of diamonds, the star-spangled sky its effulgent mirror. Sh, listen. Listen to the waves, sir, listen, my darling. Their sigh, their tickling caresses, their whispers filled with longing. Listen, they are calling: 'Cecilimisa-a-a-Misaaaaaah... Cecilimisa-Misaaaaaah...'

CECILIA: (*In raptures*). Oh...oh...darling...

PASTOR: Cecilia!

ISOLA: They call, they beckon, they are full of love. And she approaches, lady of light, bringing delight, and falls into his waiting arms —

(The Pastor, alert, is in time to prevent his daughter falling into the outstretched arms of Isola).

PASTOR: (*Sternly*). Cecilia!

ISOLA: Nothing to worry yourself about, Pastor. I'm a gentleman, I can wait. Right now we're merely going for lunch.

PASTOR: Lunch!

ISOLA: I promised Cecilimisa-Misa a treat today. You're invited of course. Although there's a passage in the Holy Book which—

CECILIA: Sorry— (*She dusts his shirt*)
ISOLA: Thanks. The famous Biblical passage informs us that three is a crowd.
CECILIA: You see, father! How he knows the Bible thoroughly.
ISOLA: Oh I don't boast about my virtues. I'm sure the Pastor knows the precise quotation.
PASTOR: I don't think I remember—
ISOLA: No? Perhaps you use the abridged version. I'm referring to the complete original Hebrew text— you read Hebrew of course—which we use in the capital, especially when the Generals come for worship. I must remember to send you a copy when I get back.
PASTOR: Yes, that's the point I wish to discuss with you, sir. I'm afraid you'll have to be leaving—
ISOLA: In another week, alas! I know how bad you feel about it. It's a shame I can't accept your hospitality for more than a fortnight. Pressing matters in the capital. But I won't forget to mention your name to the Head of State at our next briefing. (*Confidentially*) I'm not promising anything, mind, but I won't be surprised if you're promoted Bishop by government decree. That'll be something to celebrate, won't it? Ha ha. Keep your chin up! (*Laughs and pinches Pastor's cheek*). I'll be seeing you then, my good shepherd. I have a date to keep now, for this special lunch. Dear Cecilimisa-Misa. (*Wraps his arms around Cecilia and begins to lead her out. Just by the door, she runs back*).

CECILIA: Sorry— (*Brushes off speck from Pastor's shirt, then runs to join Isola, who leads her out.*)

PASTOR: Bishop! No, I mustn't think of it. What an impudent young rascal. But— No, I mustn't— But suppose it happens? Me, poor lost soul, suffering and abandoned in this God-forsaken bush town, suddenly—Bishop! Well, why not? I have served God very well all these years, why shouldn't he compensate the waste? After all, all my friends are landlords and business tycoons now, and I, I don't even own a brick. Why should I continue to wait for God's kingdom with empty hands? Oh my God, what am I saying? And yet Cecilia says he's a top official, and she can't be wrong. He'll mention my name to the Head of State! But suppose—oh, my head's going in a whirl. This scoundrel, I mean, top official from Lagos... oh sit down, old fool. Ponder a while, as the Messiah did on the mountain... reflect, reflect...

(*He has sat down, musing, on a chair. Soon he is completely lost in thought. Enter the Council Chairman, Chief James Dada Gbonmiayelobiojo, preceded by Polycap whom he is pushing forward with his cutlass. As soon as he sees the seated figure of the Pastor, who has his back to him, the Chairman comes to an abrupt stop, at the same time wheeling round in terror, afraid to look at the dreaded man).*

CHAIRMAN: Oh my head! Oh my heart! Ah, Gbonmiaiyelobiojo, everything's turning in a wild circle. I can't bear to look. Polycap, describe him to me. (*He drops *the cutlass, takes out his glasses and a newspaper which he unfolds with great agitation. As Polycap describes the sitting figure, the Chairman prepares to check off each item against a photograph in the newspaper).* Go on.

POLYCAP: (*Who is no less intimidated*). He's ...he's man, sah.

CHAIRMAN: I know he's a man! Describe him to me. The details in full.

POLYCAP: He dey wear one fine shirt.

CHAIRMAN: Don't be an idiot. Describe *him*! What he looks like.

POLYCAP: Like the Pastor sah. Like him own brother, but much uglier.

CHAIRMAN: (*With great control*). What nonsense, Polycap! This is a difficult moment, I know, but I won't permit blasphemy in my friend's house! God cannot be so wicked as to create someone uglier that the Pastor. Just describe what you see.

POLYCAP: I sorry sah. The man get...one mouth... one nose... two—yes! Two eyes. One ear, unless you count the one on the other side. But I no see that one—

CHAIRMAN: Enough! Oh my God! Ah Gbonmiaiyelobiojo, you are *fainted* to perish at the hands of imbeciles. Look, take a good look, Polycap. (*Thrusts the photograph back-wards*). Does he look like that?

POLYCAP: At all sah. He no look like newspaper.

CHAIRMAN: The photograph man! Where his name's printed. Can't you read!

POLYCAP: No sah. I no fit read.

CHAIRMAN: I know you can't read! Oh my head! What am I to do with a goat like this?

(*Forgetting himself, he hits Polycap on the head with his newspaper. Polycap's shout alerts the Pastor to their presence*).

PASTOR: Why, Polycap!

CHAIRMAN: (*Cowering closer behind Polycap*). Heavens, he's found out the name of my houseboy!

PASTOR: What are you doing here?

CHAIRMAN: I'll shut my eyes. Maybe he won't recognize me. (*Takes off his glasses quickly and shuts his eyes tight*).

PASTOR: Polycap, can't you hear me? And who's that behind you?

POLYCAP: Na my mas—

CHAIRMAN: Polycap!

POLYCAP: Nobody sah.

PASTOR: What do you mean nobody? Wait a minute, isn't that the Chairman?

CHAIRMAN: I'm finished. Give up, Gbonmiaiyelobiojo. (*Turns and bows deeply, still not looking*) Do what you will with me, your Majesty. I admit everything.

PASTOR: What game is this?

POLYCAP: (*Laughing*). Open your eyes sah. Na the Pastor.

CHAIRMAN: (*Opening his eyes cautiously*). The past—ah, it's you, Nebuchadnezzah! (*Relieved*).

PASTOR: Of course it's me, James. Who else would it be? And what game are you up to?

CHAIRMAN: I thought... I thought...
PASTOR: Anyway, I'm glad to see you. I'd just made up my mind to come and report to you the presence of—
CHAIRMAN: It's true then! He's here!
PASTOR: It's intolerable! I can't take it any longer.
CHAIRMAN: And you didn't think it *prosper* to warn me? This is what all our years of friendship come to.
PASTOR: I'm sorry; I didn't see that it concerned you.
CHAIRMAN: You didn't, Nebuchadnezzar! Since Monday!
PASTOR: I had no idea he would be staying this long.
CHAIRMAN: So what! See how you've ruined me completely!
PASTOR: Ruined *you?* When it's *my* food he's been eating!
CHAIRMAN: Who's talking of food!!!
PASTOR: I see. You mean your god-daughter, Cecilia. I admit, it's all my fault. I should have suspected he would try to seduce her.
CHAIRMAN: (*Brightening up*). Cecilia? Then that's—er, Polycap, go and wait outside. (*Polycap leaves*). I say, Nebu, that's lucky for you. So the man is *suscemptible* to women. How I wish I had a daughter now. Or—you don't think he's interested in wives too, do you? I could send Tolu— you know, my youngest wife—she's had only six sons for me. And you can help tell him her cooking is good enough to *rivalize* that of any wayside buka[10].
PASTOR: What are you saying, James? I tell you something that's causing me great distress and you make fun of it.

---

[1] *Buka:* any rough eating shed along the street.

CHAIRMAN: But I'm serious! Surely if your daughter can attract the Public Complaints Commissioner—
PASTOR: Stop! Repeat that. Who did you say?
CHAIRMAN: Your guest, the Public Complaints Commissioner of course. You said that—
PASTOR: My God, so that's who he is!
CHAIRMAN: You don't mean you don't know?
PASTOR: How sly! How utterly heartless to sneak in on me like this! All he mentioned—and to Cecilia, mind you, not to me—was that he was some official from the capital.
CHAIRMAN: And you still didn't know? What more information did you need? Ah we're all undone. All because of your dumbness. There's no hope. Unless— (*A thought strikes him. He unfolds the newspaper again and puts on his glasses.*) Nebu, describe him to me.
PASTOR: (*Completely crestfallen*). Leave it, James. I'm not good at descriptions as you know. It's too late now.
CHAIRMAN: Try all the same. It's our last chance.
PASTOR: Well, let's see. He's very brazen, almost mannerless—
CHAIRMAN: Oh my God!
PASTOR: And he has no consideration for others. He finished my last bottle of communion wine all by himself.
CHAIRMAN: For Christ's sake, Nebu, that's not what I mean! His physical *apparition*, man!
PASTOR: Repulsive. A mean-looking fellow.
CHAIRMAN: Yes, go on.
PASTOR: Short, I believe. Somewhat on the tall side.

CHAIRMAN: (*Impatiently*). Go on.
PASTOR: Medium complexion. Neither dark nor fair.
CHAIRMAN: How the hell do you expect me to tell that in a black and white photograph? Come on!
PASTOR: Well, what do you want?
CHAIRMAN: Is he, for instance ...does he have a moustache?
PASTOR: Yes. Although he's shaved it off.
CHAIRMAN: Beard?
PASTOR: He doesn't need it. His jaw is horribly dark.
CHAIRMAN: (*Giving up*). That's enough, Nebu. You're a woeful failure!
PASTOR: Why are you blaming me for his looks? I didn't create him.
CHAIRMAN: O my head! It must be him anyway. It's Solarin!
PASTOR: (*Lost again*). Lord, why hast thou forsaken me?
CHAIRMAN: We got reports this morning that the Public Complaints Commissioner is on his way here from Headquarters. What's more, he has secret instructions.
PASTOR: And you didn't warn me!
CHAIRMAN: We only got the reports this morning.
PASTOR: So what! He's been staying here for days! Oh God, this is the hour you promised, the hour of trial which every faithful believer must pass through to reach your throne. All the same, Lord, I think it's a mean trick to bring it like this, without warning —
CHAIRMAN: You're lucky, Nebuchadnezzar, you have someone to blame—
PASTOR: Do you think, James—he's been around since Monday!— do you think it's anything connected with the missing church funds?

CHAIRMAN: I sincerely hope it is, my dear friend. Anything to stop him coming round to the Council offices.

PASTOR What are you saying? After all our years of companionship, James! Ah no man is to be trusted. Good God, if you can take this cross from my head, and put it on others...(*Pointing to the Chairman*).

CHAIRMAN: (*Hastily*). I'll be back. I'm going to bring Tolu... (*He opens the door. Polycap falls in*). Really!

POLYCAP: Sah...sah... please don't bother to apologize. Na my fate.

CHAIRMAN: What impudence! I suppose it's your fever again.

POLYCAP: Yes sah, I know you'd understand. Na the yellow kind, whetin man go do? It's hereditary. My wife catch am first and passed it on to me.

CHAIRMAN: What foolishness—

POLYCAP: Na so me too I say sah. I never like yellow at all at all in my life.

CHAIRMAN: Polycap, this time you've really had it. I'm going to—

(*He moves forward, angrily, his intention clearly being to kick the grovelling Polycap. But at that moment, Isola comes in and the Chairman freezes in his uncompleted movement, one foot up and head bowed, like an acrobat.*)

CHAIRMAN: (*Stammering*). Your... Highness! Your Highness, I have the greatest honour, on behalf of the town Council, and of our entire community, the Oba, Chiefs and... and who else, damn it—yes...

ISOLA: (*Puzzled, to Pastor*). Am I interrupting anything?

PASTOR: (*Who also has his head bowed*). No, your... Majesty! It's just...

ISOLA: Majesty! Can you beat that! (*To Polycap, on the floor*). My dear fellow, were you not the one I saw leaning against the door outside just now?

CHAIRMAN: Heavens, nothing escapes him! (*Loud*). He'll pay for it, your Worship.

POLYCAP: (*Scrambling to his knees*). Na fever sah. I swear...

ISOLA: Please remain seated. I admire philosophers, especially when they're the practical kind, like me. I am pleased to meet you. I see you follow the famous dictum— 'Never stand when you can lean—' (*The Chairman hastens to lean against the nearest object*) — 'And never lean when you can sit!' (*The Chairman literally flops down*). Quite admirable! (*To Pastor, indicating Chairman*). I see your parish also employs clowns?

PASTOR: It's ...its...

ISOLA: No excuses, sir! The service of God is too precious to be taken seriously all the time.

PASTOR: Your... Highness... this is the Chairman of the local council, Chief J.D. Gbonmiaiyelobiojo.

ISOLA: Indeed! I am happy to meet a worthy representative of your people.

CHAIRMAN: I'm quite *flattened*, your, er, worship.

ISOLA: I knew you'd be. Idle people—

CHAIRMAN: It's a lie, your Majesty! I know some mischievous people have been *sprawling* rumours about me in the capital. But there's not one single truth in it. I beg you, don't allow yourself to be misled by these rascals whose fathers will never prosper in

	life. Without boasting, I can say with easy *conscientiousness* that I, Chief James Dada Gbonmiaiyelobiojo, I am the hardest working man in this whole area—
PASTOR:	What egoism! And what of the Pastor then?
ISOLA:	I was merely quoting a proverb which says that idle people—
CHAIRMAN:	I can prove it! Your... Majesty, I can demonstrate it to your satisfaction, if only you'd care not to come round to the Council Offices before you go away. I mean... oh I am undone! Look at his eyes! (*Aside, to Pastor*). Nebu, I think I'd better leave fast. He's as evil as you described him... (*Loud*). This is quite sudden, your Highness. I mean, we didn't know before of your coming but, all the same, I give you my word that you will be accorded a rousing reception worthy of such a high official of the state! I'll bring you the details myself. Please excuse me for now... (*Bowing intermittently, he begins to retreat backwards towards the door*).
PASTOR:	(*Hastily*). Wait for me! I'll see you off. (*Begins to retreat too in the same abject manner*).
ISOLA:	Oh don't go yet. (*The two men come to an abrupt halt*). I mean, the Pastor, not you, Chief Gbonmi—er, et cetera. (*The Chairman turns, to bolt out, but freezes at his voice*). I was coming to see you in fact, Pastor. I understand you want to drive me away.
PASTOR:	Me, your Majesty! Whoever could have invented such a wicked lie?

ISOLA: Dear Cecilimisa-Misa says you're tired of my presence.

PASTOR: An indiscretion of youth, Senor! She's prone to these impressions which are quite unfounded.

PASTOR: I must say it ruined my appetite.

PASTOR: I'll buy you another one! I mean... oh what am I saying? Please stay with us, your Highness. As long as you wish, the honour's ours. Feel absolutely free to take whatever you want.

ISOLA: That's a relief. You know, I almost thought you'd try to come between me and my darling Cecilimisa-Misa,

PASTOR: Ne...ne...ver! Not now, not on my life! She's ripe enough for marriage.

ISOLA: Ah, let's not rush things, Pastor. Okay? Please don't let me delay you any further.

(The two men continue to bow until they collide at the door. They pick themselves up and bolt out).

POLYCAP: Master... Master... no forget me!

ISOLA: (*Detaining him*). No, stay. Yes, remain seated. No need to tremble so much, it's infectious. If you prefer, I'll sit myself. (*Sits by him*). Now if I may ask you a question, what is your name?

POLYCAP: Po...Pol...Polycap, your—

ISOLA: I said calm yourself. What I want to discuss is in your field. I mean, philosophy.

POLYCAP: I get field sah. But I swear, I never meet this woman there. The only Philo I know be my brother's wife, and...

ISOLA: That's all right, Polycap. Just tell me, in simple words, what you overheard just now when you were looking through the keyhole. And remember, no lies.

POLYCAP: Sah...sah. I...I no fit... Master go kill me!...
ISOLA: Talk! Let me warm you that I am capable of viciousness myself. So don't waste my time. (*Takes out some Naira note from his pocket and shows him*). It's my last note. But I have a feeling that the information's important and many explain the strange behaviour of the two men. (*Gives him*). Now, talk!

(*Polycap gives a yell of joy, leaps and crashes into a posture of prostration. He begins to roll on the floor, alternate cheeks to the ground*).

POLYCAP: Master... this is for me! You don kill me!
ISOLA: All right, all right. Now tell me what you heard, quickly.
POLYCAP: (*Subsiding, licking the note*). It's like this ... No spare them sah! I beg you in the name of your mama, make you punish the Pastor, and make you jail the Chairman.!
ISOLA: Me? But—.
POLYCAP: Them be thieves proper! That is what they were discussing. How them go deceive you so you no go find out before you go away! So I beg you, sah, in the name of God no spare these wicked robbers at all at all !
ISOLA: I won't. But tell me, why do you think I can do it? Why are they afraid of me?
POLYCAP: Ah everybody here don hear of you sah, the way you dey manner all those people for Ibadan and Lagos! No to you be Mr Solarin, the Commissioner of Complaint?
ISOLA: Ah! How did you know?

POLYCAP: We don see your anthem for radio. My pickens dey sing am sotay! 'For dis corner, you dey there... for dat corner, you dey there!' Ah, Master, you no go die! You know, all dis morning, my Master and him friends, Councillor Abeni and Kaokudi, Chief Force is Force, the Dokita and the Judge, they meet and begin to halla because they hear say you dey come. Ha ha, they no know say you don arrove already! You too cunning sha! The Pastor too, he begin to shake sake of the church money wey lost last month. Ah sah, you too terrible. The fear wey you give everybody! And all because they don hear say you no dey take bribery and corruption from nobody—ah, that remind me. Take care sah. They go try to bribe you.

ISOLA: Who?

POLYCAP: All of them. The Pastor. The Chief of Magistrate. The Councillors, all of them.

ISOLA: You think so?

POLYCAP: Na so dem they do every time somebody come from Lagos.

ISOLA: Excellent!

POLYCAP: Pardon, sah?

ISOLA: I mean... Polycap, you must make sure that they try to bribe me.

POLYCAP: Whetin sah!!!

ISOLA: Yes. It's like this: I want to set them a trap, so I can catch them red-handed. Then I'll have them thrown in prison. Won't you like that?

POLYCAP: Very much sah. Na the thing I dey pray for self.

ISOLA: Good. As soon as you get back, go straight to Chief Gbonmi—etcetera. I mean, the Chairman. Tell him I have noticed some odd goings-on in the town and I'd like to see him and his councillors as soon as possible. Go now.

(Exit Polycap, licking the naira note).

ISOLA: (*Striding about the room*). How funny! How fortunate! So they think I am the Public Complaints Commissioner! And naturally they are loaded with sins and fear. Well, let them come to purge themselves. I am sure it'll be a mutually beneficial exercise. Ah, talk of walking into a gold mine! What will they say when I get back! I must enter this into my diary! Yes, straight into my diary!

Exits. End of PART TWO.

PART THREE

(Same place, the Pastor's sitting-dining room. Later, in the evening. Stage is empty for a few seconds after the lights come on. Then Lamidi's head appears cautiously at the window. It is masked, but mainly symbolically, i.e. not so much as to prevent recognition by audience.)

LAMIDI: *(Looking in).* All clear, Lemomu.
(His head disappears from window at the same time as Lemomu, similarly masked, enters through the outside door, on tiptoe. He begins to search around. Soon Lamidi joins him. They each take regular peeps out through the window).

LAMIDI: You really think it's here?

LEMOMU: Use your head, Lamidi. Where else could it be?

LAMIDI: I don't know. We've gone through the other rooms and found nothing. Except for these love letters. *(Begins to read).* 'My darling Nebuchadnezzar...'

LEMOMU: Forget the letters. The Pastor's only human and if the women are willing— *(Snatches the letter).*

LAMIDI: Yes, but they are married! *(Reads another one).* 'Lovely dated ...'

LEMOMU: So what, you bush man. *(Snatches the letter).* It's the modern taste: the married ones are the most lonely, needing religious consolation. Anyway, forget it. It's the missing funds that we're interested in.

LAMIDI: One thing is sure: he hasn't had any chance to dispose of the money. It's still somewhere in the house.

LEMOMU: And I'm convinced it's in this room. It's the last place anyone would think of searching.

LAMIDI: Well— (*A cough at the door. Lamidi dodges behind the dining table. Lemomu, not so lucky, is hurrying forward towards the same place, running in a crouch, when he is arrested by the voice of the Pastor, coming in. He stops dead, taking a rapid decision. By the time the Pastor notices, Lemomu is already in a fixed rigid posture, like a statue*).

PASTOR: (*At the door*). Come in quick, Baba Fawomi, while they're out. I'll keep watch at the— (*Sees Lemomu*).

BABA FAWOMI: (*Entering*). What is it? Ah, a sculpture. Where did you buy it?

PASTOR: I don't keep idols, Baba Fawomi! (*Goes and inspects it*). This must be Cecilia's idea of a joke. The way she carries on these days, you wouldn't know she is my daughter. Unless— (*Looks again at Lemomu, and gives him kick. Lemomu falls and then springs back into place, startling the Pastor*). It's on springs too!

BABA FAWOMI: I'll advice you to leave it alone. I must say your daughter has a good taste. It's a beautiful work of art. So life-like, you'd think it was breathing!

PASTOR: You don't think ... that, that the Commissioner brought it here to catch me?

BABA FAWOMI: Don't be a fool. I am here! I'll deal with him, just leave it all to me. (*Deposits his things on Lemomu's head*). I've dealt with stronger ones before.

PASTOR: I'll keep watch at the door.

BABA FAWOMI: (*Spreading his paraphernalia on Lemomu's head*). Orunmila is great, but Ifa has never been known yet to talk on a dry throat.

PASTOR: Later, Baba. I've sent Cecilia to the shops. The Commissioner finished the last wine bottle all by himself yesterday.

BABA FAWOMI: Well, I hope you realize this exercise is going to cost you a lot.

PASTOR: Any price, I told you, Baba. Oh I know I'm a sinner but I was hoping to reform before the Last Judgement. And now this Commissioner! He must not find out about those funds. And I promise you that, when I become Bishop—

BABA FAWOMI: You'll forget me then! You'll go to more 'sophisticated' diviners. It's happened before.

PASTOR: Not with me, I swear. God is my witness. I'll enhance your status. Please hurry up.

BABA FAWOMI: Well, I only mentioned the fees because you complained so much last time. The trouble I took dispelling the suspicions of your congregation about the missing funds! Yet when it was all over, when another person had been jailed for it, you became difficult, even though what I demanded for Ifa was not up to one tenth of the stolen money. I don't like my clients misbehaving when it comes to settling accounts.

PASTOR: Forgive me, Baba Fawomi. It was the Devil. But I promise, I'll more than compensate this time. Please hurry up.

BABA FAWOMI: (*Ready with his charms now*). Right, turn your back.

(*The Pastor turns towards the door. Baba Fawomi, chanting, shaking his opele, walks slowly round the room. Nothing that he sings is recognizably from Ifa, but the noises are impressive enough, especially at those moments when small valuable objects in the room mysteriously disappear into his bag or the folds of his agbada. Lamidi is kept dodging round the table to avoid being seen*).

BABA FAWOMI: (*Stopping abruptly*). I don't like it, Pastor. I don't like it. This man is strong.

PASTOR: (*Beginning to turn, and so almost discovering Lamidi, who is in a conspicuous position at that moment*). What—

BABA FAWOMI: Don't turn round, please! (*Lamidi is saved*). No, sir! Don't imperil yourself. Leave the fight to Ifa and the stubborn devils. (*Chants, then shouts suddenly*). Move, you! (*Everybody starts, including Lemomu, who however quickly recovers and resumes, unnoticed, his frozen posture*). No, sir, I warn you, don't turn your back! (*Shouts again*). Move out of the way, you disgusting spirits of the dark! (*Lamidi is again kept dodging round table*). Oh-ho, you think you'll find where the funds are hidden? Ehn?

PASTOR: Baba ... Baba ... shouldn't I lock the windows?

BABA FAWOMI: Sh! Don't interrupt. (*Chants, then goes to Pastor*). Pastor, it's no use. I've got to deceive them. Have you any money on you? No don't look, I beg you. Just hand it over.

PASTOR: Let me see. (*He brings out some bills and wants to count, but Baba Fawomi snatches the money*).

BABA FAWOMI: No time to count. Quick! I'll pass it on to them and see. The spirits he's brought here are some of the greediest of the Other World. (*Runs back and resumes his chant. Lemomu, trying to creep away, is caught in a new position*). Move, I say! The Pastor must climb to that throne of Bishops! Tell me nothing of those funds!

PASTOR: The windows…really…I'll shut them! (*Moves*).

BABA FAWOMI: What! And trap the vermin inside? Ah look, see what you've done! I told you not to look back, didn't I? Now it's all unstuck! (*Sits down in disgust*).

PASTOR: (*Looking at Lemomu*). The sculpture…Baba! The sculpture, it's moved!

BABA FAWOMI: (*Not looking*). I told you! Now all the devils will be unleashed! Oh, too bad.

PASTOR: (*Crestfallen*). What…what can be done now?

BABA FAWOMI: Nothing but to start all over again. Ah, if only you'll listen to me. This thing takes too much energy out of me each time. You may not realize it, but I'm growing old. My strength isn't quite what it used to be. (*Takes off his heavy agbada and hangs it on Lemomu*). Well, to work. I don't see how I can abandon a friend at a crucial hour of need. But no more disobedience!

PASTOR: I promise.

BABA FAWOMI: I only hope you've still got some money in the house. And I really mean money, not like those few scraps of paper you've just wasted. I would have lent you, but you know, after the sacrifices to Ifa…

PASTOR: (*Searching in his other pocket*). It's all right. I have something here.

BABA FAWOMI: (*Wise to his game now*). No, that still won't do.

PASTOR: No? Well, let me see again. (*Searches in his breast pocket*). Here we are.

BABA FAWOMI: And how much is that? (*Turning to collect his things*). Look, if you're not serious—

PASTOR: Please!

BABA FAWOMI: I'm ready to help you, but you have to be willing to help yourself a little. You've got how many pockets? (*Patting him all over for pockets*). Empty them! Oh the blindness of mortals! What a pity you cannot see the terrible spirits the man has brought along with him! Why do you think he's been able to operate so successfully all these years without a scratch? I tell you, the man is a terror! In your own interest, Nebu, in your own interest, buy them off! A bribe is a bribe, and all government officials are *suscemptible* whether spirits or humans! It's the size of it that counts—

(*During the speech, while Baba Fawomi is searching the Pastor's pockets and emptying them of money, Lamomu has been edging towards the door, with all the Ifa priest's belongings on him. He makes it out of the room, at the same moment that the Pastor turns. However, Lamidi, who has also been crawling forward towards the door, is in time to take the place of the sculpture. Neither the Pastor nor Baba notices anything amiss. In fact, Baba Fawomi, in pretended indifference, tucks the bills of money into Lamidi's gaping mouth*).

PASTOR: (*Becoming suspicious as he goes towards door*). Baba... the sculpture! It's—

BABA FAWOMI: What about the sculpture, will you leave it alone! Why, is this a moment to appreciate the beauty of art! Nebu, please go to the door and turn your back. I have other business waiting at home. (*Pastor turns his back*). Now you demons, I am your Master! I shall—

CECILIA: (*Calling from outside*). Papa! Father!

(*Pastor, horrified, gestures quickly to Baba Fawomi to hide behind dining-table*).

PASTOR: (*Trying to meet daughter at the door*). Ah Cecilia, I—

CECILIA: Let me come in father, I have good news for you!

PASTOR: Come and—

CECILIA: (*Brushing his shoulder so that he steps back a little*). Sorry.

PASTOR: Come and tell me outside.

CECILIA: Oh you have no idea! (*She dances past him into the room*). How happy I am. Father I have sinned!

PASTOR: God forbid!

CECILIA: I have sinned. You will be angry. You will never forgive me. (*Folds her hands round his neck and whirls him round in a dance*). I am so happy!

PASTOR: Really, Cecilia, control yourself. Tell me the worst.

CECILIA: You can't imagine it. Father!

PASTOR: Just tell me what you've done.

CECILIA: It's unpardonable.

PASTOR: Say it so I can—
CECILIA: I didn't ask your permission. I sinned!
PASTOR: But let me hear it?
CECILIA: (*Brushing off his lapels*). Sorry—Oh father, this is my happiest moment. I'm in love!
PASTOR: In love! This is a crisis. Cecilia, I'll stand by you. I'll call the catechist and we'll arrange a Holy Communion. You'll fall out of it again.
CECILIA: Don't you understand, father? It's with the Complaints Commissioner.
CECILIA: Solarin?
CECILIA: We're planning to marry soon, so he can ask for your consent as soon as possible after our honeymoon. We'll have six children, four boys and two girls. Or maybe seven, the magic number. Then—
PASTOR: I give my consent, Cecilia! What! You've saved my life! You've brought me honour. Ah, if only your mother were alive to see this moment! I'll arrange a Holy Communion at once to bless it.
CECILIA: I knew you'd understand. You're so wonderful! Come, come and see—

(*She drags father to the window. Baba Fawomi quickly dodges to another position as Lamidi escapes, unnoticed. As Cecilia goes on, the Pastor makes signs to Baba Fawomi to run out, but the latter does not understand the message*).

CECILIA: See, father, how even nature celebrates the occasion. The moon, the night, like a walk along the Marina. Ah, the golden-yellow lights blinking like glow-worms!...

(At last Baba Fawomi understands the message and begins to crawl towards the door).

CECILIA: ...You should see the sea then, my friend, oh the marvel of that enchanted moment, spread out like a bed of diamonds, the star-spangled sky its effulgent mirror. Sh, listen to the waves— (*The Pastor is completely frozen as he watches Baba Fawomi*). Their sigh, their tickling caresses, their whispers filled with longing. (*Cecilia, noticing her father's fixed stare, turns to see. Baba Fawomi freezes into the same posture as the 'sculpture' that has disappeared*). Father, what's the matter?

PASTOR: (*Hastily*). Nothing. I was listening to you, my dear. How beautiful. 'The night ...and so on'. Carry on.

CECILIA: You weren't listening. I have passed that sentence. Anyway—Sorry. (*She wipes off sweat off his brow*). I'll go back a bit. (*As she continues her speech, Baba Fawomi, without leaving his position, renews the silent but heated conversation, over his missing properties. The Pastor begins carefully to stir his daughter towards the door, without allowing her to turn her head*).

CECILIA: ...Their sigh, their tickling caresses, their whispers filled with longing. Listen, they're calling—Father!

PASTOR: (*Recovering again, as he stirs her out*). Yes, I'm listening. It's like the Book of Job, absolutely enthralling. 'Their tickling filled with whispers ...!' Ah, I'm so happy, my daughter. We must celebrate, yes, yes...!

(They go out. Baba Fawomi rises and begins to search round the room).

BABA FAWOMI: *(Angry).* I have said it again and again, never trust these Christians. But no, I get taken in every time. Sculpture! I should have been suspicious. Ah Ifa, see how the man has made an idiot of me. But I'll have my vengeance! I'll draw blood! I'll— *(Approaching footsteps send him dodging back behind the table. Enter Isola, in high spirits, with a diary and a pen in his hand).*

ISOLA: Ah, dear diary, you've never had it so good! What! The news and gossips you have eaten today, ehn, greedy thing! You want more? No doubt. Well, how do you take this: I, Isola Oriebora—sh! Forget that! *(Looks round)* I, the one they dismissed as no good, I am being courted! Yes, someone wants to marry me! Well, not me but my new self. For I am now the Public Complaints Commissioner, by popular consent in this strange town! Ah, what comedy! I can't tell you half of all that's been happening. But I am being courted, by no less a person than the beautiful, pretty, attractive, lovely, stunning, devastating—ah, shall I go on?...gorgeous, amorous, radiant, captivating and delicious! Delicious Cecilimisa-Misaaaaaah, daughter of the most Right Reverend Pastor Nebcadnezar Ifagbemi! And I am going to marry her—some time in the future. First, the engagement, which I have promised her will be ...well, let's not hurry things. We must get to know each other properly. And the people of this town! Out of a fairy tale. I don't believe any of them is sane. Some general epidemic of the brain. However, Commissioner I am, see me! (*Laughs and begins to strut round the room, leaving his diary on table*). Now to prepare to welcome them, my visitors. For I know night is their best time of call. For all the intrigues that ruin in this nation. And the machinations which break all our wasted young lives. But they'll pay for it, the Chairman and his comrades. (*Remembering something, he hastens to the diary and reads. Assured, he drops the diary again and laughs*). Better and better! Who says life's not like a prostitute! I leave Lagos, fleeing from debts, an imminent probe, and a landlord on the war-path, and what do I run into? Robbers! Just like that, my friends! I have to walk ten kilometres in the bush, searching for the next town, and where do I land? In a vicarage! Tell me, in the circumstances what could be better? Who can forget the long-reputed charity of the church? Especially when there's a beautiful, suppressed girl who takes a look at your wretched condition and promptly falls headlong in love? With such around, the church just simply has to fulfil its promise of charity to all the forsaken! So here I am trying to put on some flesh again and think out my best way of facing the coming probe with an empty pocket. And what happens again? I'm to be mistaken for Solarin, the Public Complaints Commissioner. A good man, except that he's one of those who should never have left paradise. Poor Solarin, how I wish you were here to see me! I'm going to help your image today by correcting the worst of your natural failings! I'll recreate a Solarin very much in the national image. And when I get back to Lagos, let any bastard dare to put me on trial! (*Laughs*).

(*Enter Madam Gbomiayelobiojo, pushed in by her husband. The latter gives a low bow and retreats backwards out of sight. She is dressed almost like a tart, with a lot of jewellery and make-up*).

ISOLA: Nobody knocks in this house? (*Tolu, trembling, does not answer*). Well, it doesn't matter. Please take a seat, Madam— (*She lifts one of the chairs, still trembling*). No, no. I mean, sit down, please and tell me how I can help you. Don't be so frightened, madam.

TOLU: (*With a deep curtsey : her accent shows very limited education*). I yam notu frighten, sah.

ISOLA: I... beg your pardon?

TOLU: (*In an obviously rehearsed coquettish posture, and quoting*). I yam Tolu. A trial will convince you.

ISOLA: (*The lady-killer now, drawing closer*). Oh delighted! What an entrancing name! To-o-o-lu! Let me take your hand, my angel. Ah, what superb fingers. (*Tries to kiss them*).

TOLU: (*Snatching back her hand in terror*). I beggi you. Please, sah I beggi you. Do notu eat me!

ISOLA: No, no, Tolu. I just wanted—

TOLU: (*On her knees, her hands far behind her*). I beggi you. Please, sah, I beggi you.

ISOLA: (*Impassioned now*). Oh really! Do not condemn me to perpetual fire in the heaven of potsherds. What, those golden knees should never touch the dust! For the fate of queens is to ride the air like goddesses. Oh please rise, my queen, and suffer that I, your poor slave, sing to you with my limited craft the boundless splendour of your heavenly abode. (*Leads her, mesmerized, to the window. As he becomes absorbed in his lyrical speech, Baba Fawomi rises, seizes the diary, and runs out unnoticed*). Goddess, we swoon here as we watch you ride the earth, astride the moon, your splendid horse. Along the Marina, the whisperings of young lovers invoke you, for you are the only one, the same one to whom they sing. You pause, hearing the passionate supplications, and gently you shake your garments, goddess. And that single gesture unloosens a thousand diamonds into the night sky. Goddess— (*He falls onto his knees*). I am consumed by that fire lit by your glance, whose sparks illumine the night. I am aflame with love. For you.

TOLU: (*Trying to escape*). Esikiissi sah! Esi-kissi sah, you willi dirty your trouser...!

ISOLA: Let me learn my fate, goddess—will it be life or death?

(*Cecilia appears from the bedroom, unnoticed*).

TOLU: Sah... they willi be beating me for this. Jamisi willi annoy at me. I beggi you, stand now.

ISOLA: Only you can redeem me, goddess. A word— and I am saved or lost for ever

CECILIA: Darling! You said those words to me!
ISOLA: Cecilimisa...!
CECILIA: Don't touch me! (*She sobs*)
TOLU: (*Escaping*). I thanki you, Cecilia. I yam running to my shopu. (*Exits*).
ISOLA: Darling, you know you're the only one I love in my life. Ah Cecilimisa-Misa, remember, I promised you the Marina. As soon as I—Cecilia!

(*He is cut short by the sight of Cecilia approaching, the Chairman's abandoned cutlass in her hand. There is a chase round the room. The Chairman puts his head in, sees what is happening, and quickly dodges out of sight. From the bedroom also, the Pastor enters and quickly withdraws, making the sign of the cross. At last Isola falls on his knees*).

ISHOLA: All right, kill me. It's our first quarrel, and I am willing to die for it.
CECILIA: (*Becoming brutal in her anger, breaks into pidgin, all the docility gone*). Die whetin? Who go give you chance to die like that? You don marry me, or you think I go just allow you to escape? You never die man. You go marry me first. And you get only two seconds to decide.
ISOLA: Of course, of course I'll marry you.
CECILIA: *Yeye*[1] man! Anyway I thank you for proposal. I accept. Now take this ring (*Brings it out from her bra*). Slip it on my finger. (*He does*). Well, now that I am engaged to you, what are you—
ISOLA: Engaged!
CECILIA: I announced it already to my father more than an

---

[1] *Yeye*: literally, 'useless', 'worthless'.

	hour ago. Well, what are you waiting for? Won't you kiss me? (*He approaches, while she smiles and drops the cutlass*). I'll make you so happy darling. I promise. The wedding's for tomorrow afternoon.
ISOLA:	(*Jumps back in shock*). What, Cecilia!
CECILIA:	Cecilimisa-Misa. I prefer that from you, dear.
ISOLA:	Yes…er, Cecilimisa-Misa. It's too sudden. I mean, tomorrow afternoon! No, I've got to prepare. I must tell my parents.
CECILIA:	You told me you're an orphan—
ISOLA:	Yes, but—Listen, I've got relatives. I've got friends. Besides, there's a way about these things …
CECILIA:	What's the fuss? You're Solarin. Everybody knows you don't respect conventions.
ISOLA:	Yes, yes, I know. But … my dear, there's something else, something more grievous… I'm married.
CECILIA:	(*Laughing*). Look at this man! Of course I knew you were married.
ISOLA:	You knew!
CECILIA:	Well, I guessed it. I know it won't bother you either. Besides, anyone can see you're old enough to re-marry.
ISOLA:	Cecilia, I tell you —
CECILIA:	Look, the Chairman and his friends will soon be here. You've got to be ready to meet them. Come, I'll make you a splendid meal while you wait.

BLACKOUT. End of PART THREE.

PART FOUR

(Same place. A few minutes later. Sitting are the Chief magistrate, the Chief Medical Officer, Councillors for Education and Works and for Co-operatives and Agriculture, and the Price Control Officer. The Chairman, anxious, is striding about. He listens at the door.)

CHAIRMAN: He'll soon finish his meal, and that's a consolation. Remember, we're all in the same leaking boat and we'll either sink or float together. I don't want to sink. I've told you, he's a brutal man. That he has chosen to have his supper in the kitchen, right off the stoves, is alarming enough. But I'm telling you, I saw him attack Tolu with his teeth. And she was only going to sell him some ... er, face powder. So let's not say or do anything to provoke him to *cannibality*. Now let's go through it again carefully. When he enters, what do we do?

COUNCILLOR FOR EDUCATION: We fall flat on our bellies.

COUNCILLOR FOR COOPERATIVES: No, you coconut head. That's for you men. We are to curtsey.

CHAIRMAN: That's all right. The men prostrate, and the women go on their knees. What do we say then?

ALL: *(In various accents).* *Soyez la bienvenue, vot'* Excellency!

CHAIRMAN: Again, please. And try to remember that it's French, not one of our remote dialects.

(They repeat the greeting, with no improvement).

CHAIRMAN: Well, well, I suppose he'll understand. He's a cultured man. Ah Gbonmiayelobiojo, to be saddled with these primitives! After the greeting what next?

PRICE CONTROL OFFICER: The song. (*Singing, a high falsetto*). 'For he's a jolly good—'

CHAIRMAN: No, no. Together. Let's all take it together, softly.

ALL: (*Singing, in audible discordance*). 'For he's a jolly good fellow, for he's a jolly—'

CHAIRMAN: (*Wiping his forehead*). That will do, that will do. Lucky it's not the national anthem, or you'd all have been *arranged* for treason. I said, sing, not reproduce the hawing of toads. Ah, Gbomiayelobiojo, uneasy lies the head! I think we'd better leave out the singing, ehn?

COUNCILLOR FOR EDUCATION: JDG, I still maintain that we should try something more ***positive***. You know, a little kola...

CHAIRMAN: And end up where? You know, if I didn't like you, I'd let you go ahead with it. You talk as if you didn't know the reputation of the man. He'll kick up a storm. He'll put it in all the headlines! And where do you think you'll be afterwards?

COUNCILLOR FOR COOPERATIVES: Don't stop him, JDG. Some people are born to end in Kirikiri[12].

COUNCILLOR FOR EDUCATION: Listen—

CHIEF MAGISTRATE: I'm in support of Force is Force. Whatever the man is, he is still a government official, like all of us. In my court, we always take the money into consideration to know who is guilty or who is to be freed. It's a question of finding what his price is.

---

[12] *Kirikiri:* the name of a notorious maximum security prison in Lagos.

COUNCILLOR FOR EDUCATION: And the best approach would be on individual basis. He'll be more amenable to private arrangements then. But with a whole army like this, nothing will be achieved. That's when he'll remember his public reputation and use it to kick us in the face.

DOCTOR: I agree. (*Coughing*). Secrecy helps. You remember that ... that excuse me, it was how we broke the strike by the junior workers in the hospital. The leaders walked in one after another and... and, excuse me, collected their envelopes. And that was the end of the strike.

CHAIRMAN: (*Helpless*). Yes, but this is the Complaints Commissioner!

COUNCILLOR FOR EDUCATION: Let's give it a try, JDG. We'll approach him one by one with our different envelopes—and we can agree on a uniform sum, say, a contribution towards his travelling expenses and so forth.

CHAIRMAN: All right then. Ayo, you will go first.

CHIEF MAGISTRATE: Why me? It's an honour that belongs more appropriately to the Chairman.

CHAIRMAN: Let's not stand on rights now, my friends. In fact I think the best thing would be for me to go last, you know, like a father after his children. I've always been fond of the paternal image. If you can't go, Ayo, then Force is Force will lead the way. His rank is important, as the Councillor in charge of the town's enlightenment.

COUNCILLOR FOR EDUCATION: I can't, my friends. Really I can't. I've had an unfortunate education. I went through school in those days when examination leakages were famous. And I never made the University like our dear colleague here, who even had the singular fortune to be taught by the great Awo and Zik of Africa. And what gift of eloquence when she talks! A rare combination of parrot and nightingale! Not to talk of the elegance of her slender throat, which will just charm away the Commissioner—

PRICE CONTROL OFFICER: I hope you will not listen to him. Slender throat indeed! Everybody knows I am ugly, and I've got vulgar manners. And all that talk about eloquence is pure rubbish. Just because I picked up some words from playing Scrabble, and overheard some gossip about Zik and Awo. Nonsense. Have I been in Lagos before? If anyone should go first, it's clearly the Chief Magistrate.

ALL: (*Crowding round the Chief Magistrate*). Please go! Brave the Rubicon! Deliver the first blow! Show you're a hero!

CHIEF MAGISTRATE: (*Struggling*). Let go! Let go of me, I say! We'll all face him together!

(*Sound of singing, from the inner rooms. Voice unmistakably that of Isola. The men freeze, then lose their nerves. They rush for the door, pushing and screaming. Isola enters, humming a song. With him is Cecilia*).

ISOLA: (*Looking around*). That's funny. I could have sworn I heard voices.

CECILIA: I thought so too, my darling. I'm sure they have arrived. I'll go and look out—

(The outside door opens, and the Chief Magistrate comes in. He is obviously being pushed from behind. He stands trembling at the door. Once or twice, as Isola speaks, he tries to run out, but is again pushed back into the room).

ISOLA: Ah, they're beginning to come. All the better, if they arrive one by one. My dear, you'll have to excuse us. That was an excellent meal, especially eaten like that in the kitchen with no ceremony. It would have been lovely for us to sit and digest together, but now official business is calling. You know my reputation: never mix business with pleasure. (*Slaps her buttocks*). Go in, but stay awake for me, eh? The moon will soon be full, as I ordered. (*She leaves*).

CHIEF MAGISTRATE: (*His eyes turned to heaven*). Oh Lord, oh Lord! I know I've made careless remarks about you before but, as one judge to another, you can't let me down. I'll take the first step, take the second for me. (*Steps forward*). Your Excellency, I have the honour to present myself—Ayokanmi Olawale Olaitan, Chief Magistrate of the district, Chairman of the local Police Committee, founder of the local Civil Defence Corps, and Life Patron of the Boys' Brigade.

ISOLA: Do sit down. So you are the Magistrate here?

CHIEF MAGISTRATE: (*Not sitting*). Yes, sir. I was promoted to that position some years back after due recommendation by the Fraternity. I've always been faithful to the cult's charter and paid my dues regularly. Unlike these modern boys who think because they have a University degree and—

ISOLA: I see, I see. I guess you find your position ...profitable?

CHIEF MAGISTRATE: Only last year I was recommended for one of the national honours. Of course I didn't get it, this town being what it is, a hive of plotters and jealous backbiters. (*Aside*). This money is burning a hole through my hand!

ISOLA: Well, I'm sorry to hear it. But I'm not surprised. In my job I get to hear a number of similar complaints. It even gets boring— (*Sneezes*).

CHIEF MAGISTRATE: (*Thrusting his hand forward, with envelope, but looking away*). Oh Lord, here it is. Let me ... your Excellency, let me offer you a handkerchief ...

ISOLA: What's that?

CHIEF MAGISTRATE: (*Shaken, drops envelope*). Oh, nothing ... I mean, a... a handkerchief ...

ISOLA: You dropped an envelope! (*Picks it up*).

CHIEF MAGISTRATE: Me sir? Impossible. It's a handkerchief. (*Aside*). Oh Lord, bail me out!

ISOLA: Why, it's full of currency. Brand new notes.

CHIEF MAGISTRATE: (*Aside*). It's all over now. It's the firing block for me.

ISOLA: Well, I wonder—could you lend me some of this?

CHIEF MAGISTRATE: Lend, sir? Take it all! (*Ecstatic*). All of it ... I make you a present of it, your Excellency!

ISOLA: I'm very low in cash—you must have heard of my luck with the robbers on my way here. And as I've just got engaged, I'll be needing a lot of money.

CHIEF MAGISTRATE: Engaged, your Excellency?

ISOLA: Yes, to the Pastor's daughter.

CHIEF MAGISTRATE: What !

ISOLA: The wedding's tomorrow. I'll send you a cheque as soon as I get back.

CHIEF MAGISTRATE: Don't mention it, sir! Keep the money; it'll be my wedding present. Please accept my congratulations! (*Rising*). Your Excellency will have a lot to do, so I will not presume to disturb you further with my humble presence. I wish you a happy married life. (*Goes out hastily*).

ISOLA: (*Pocketing the money*). This is not a bad way to start! But I must start planning my escape from here. I have only this night. It won't be easy, the girl watches every move. Her love for me is so strong that it's like being in an iron cage.

(*Enter the Price Control Officer*).

PRICE CONTROL OFFICER: (*Curtseying*). I have the honour to present myself. Mrs Abeni Mailo, daughter of the late Reverend Durosimi, the famous pianist-composer, graduate of Isabatudeen Secondary Modern School, Ajilete. I am the Price Control Officer here.

ISOLA: Welcome. I've heard of you. I'm glad to meet the daughter of such a famous person, the late Reverend Mailo—

PRICE CONTROL OFFICER: Reverend Durosimi, your Highness. I am Mrs Mailo.

ISOLA: Of course, of course! Madam, I see you have a superb taste in dresses. And what expensive earrings! Your job is—lucrative?

PRICE CONTROL OFFICER: I...don't know what you mean, your Highness. This is a vicious country. People are always making up stories. Half the national diet is gossip. I assure you that I don't make more out of my job than my colleagues in other towns.

ISOLA: (*Aside*). This one may be difficult, but let's try... Madam, you've heard of my engagement, no doubt?

PRICE CONTROL OFFICER: Engagement?

ISOLA: To Cecilia, the Pastor's daughter.

PRICE CONTROL OFFICER: But ... that's extremely lucky. For the Pastor.

ISOLA: The wedding's tomorrow. Very short notice, but that's me. I pass for an eccentric, but that's the only way to get things done. I've heard several complaints since I came, from the market women and the beer sellers, but to tell you a secret, it's quite possible this wedding will keep me too busy to attend to those complaints. I'm counting on my friends to make the wedding successful.

PRICE CONTROL OFFICER: Your Highness... I hope you'll count me as one of your friends. Let me prove it with this, if your Highness will do me the honour of accepting? (*Brings out an envelope, which she hands over*). And this, to make the friendship closer, if it's not too much presumption? (*Hands another envelope*).

ISOLA: Oh thanks, thanks very much! I'm lavish with my friendships when I see the proof! Why, I've been known to forgive my bitterest enemies when they're willing to pay for it. Consider yourself a close friend of the family from this moment, Mrs Mailo.

PRICE CONTROL OFFICER: You honour me, your highness... er, will there be any orders?

ISOLA: Orders? What orders?

PRICE CONTROL OFFICER: I mean, concerning those traders...?

ISOLA: They'll all be detained. Rumour-mongering is a most heinous crime, especially against conscientious officials.

PRICE CONTROL OFFICER: Thank you, your Highness! In that case I shall not presume to disturb you further with my presence. Goodnight. (*She curtseys and leaves*).

ISOLA: Three envelopes already! This should go into my diary! The characters are behaving exactly as I guessed they would when I went to spy them out this afternoon with dear Cecilia! (*Searching*). Damn, where could I have left the diary? Anyway—(*Shouts*). Next!

(*A pathetic scene. The Councillor for Education rolls in on his belly, followed by the Councillor for Cooperatives who is on her knees, both hands extended forward in supplication*).

ISOLA: Well! This is an innovation!

BOTH: (*Starting together*). Your Excellency— (*They stop*).

COUNCILLOR FOR EDUCATION: Go on. After you.

COUNCILLOR FOR COOPERATIVES: No, you go on.

COUNCILLOR FOR EDUCATION: It's always ladies first.

COUNCILLOR FOR COOPERATIVES: Your...Lordship, I...He is the Councillor for Education.

COUNCILLOR FOR EDUCATION: Introduce yourself! I'll do mine myself!

COUNCILLOR FOR COOPERATIVES: I am... your Lordship, with all...all humility... I am...(*Pathetic*) No, I can't do it, Force is Force, I can't!

ISOLA: Are you Force is Force?

COUNCILLOR FOR EDUCATION: Don't mind her, your Excellency! It's a nickname. Who am I? I have no force at all! My name is Chief Funso Fowolu, F.F., which they have turned into Force is Force to ruin me. I am a poor, humble and abiding servant of the people, ready to do your bidding.

ISOLA: Well, sit down. I'm sure you'll find it more comfortable. You, I presume, are the Councillor for Co-operatives, in charge of the OFN program.

COUNCILLOR FOR COOPERATIVES: (*Abjectly*). I can't deny it, your Lordship.

ISOLA: I'm sure you've both heard the news?

BOTH: (*Reciting*). We wish you a happy married life.

ISOLA: Thank you, and let's stop beating about the bush. Hand over your envelopes.

COUNCILLOR FOR EDUCATION: (*Taken aback*). I...beg your pardon!? (*Recovering*). Ah, yes, of course, your Excellency. Kaokudi, after you.

COUNCILLOR FOR COOPERATIVES: Why me first? Why not you?

COUNCILLOR FOR EDUCATION: All right, I'll start. (*Gives envelopes*). Your Excellency, let me wish you many happy returns. Oh, I'm sorry! I mean, congratulations. Your turn, Kudi.

COUNCILLOR FOR COOPERATIVES: (*Giving her own envelopes*). A fertile marriage, your Lordship.

COUNCILLOR FOR EDUCATION: Is that all?

COUNCILLOR FOR COOPERATIVES: What do you mean?

COUNCILLOR FOR EDUCATION: Well, give way. (*With great bombast*) That was only the first instalment, your Excellency. Please, do me the honour of accepting the second. (*Gives envelope*). Remember, it is from the Councillor for Education, Chief Funso Fowolu, alias Force is…er, Chief Funso Fowolu. (*looking maliciously at Kaokudi, who stands by, apparently speechless*). And here's the third instalment from, this time, the Councillor for Works, also Chief Funso Fowolu. And finally, from both of me, a fourth instalment, to wish you a happy and prosperous married life.

ISOLA: I say, this is quite generous! What did you say your name is again?

COUNCILLOR FOR EDUCATION: Chief Funso Fowolu! Think nothing of it, your Excellency. It's little, where the heart is full of love and devotion to your eminent personality. We're not tight-fisted like certain officials…

COUNCILLOR FOR COOPERATIVES: (*Who has been undoing her long cloth wallet*). I shall now start, your Lordship, to congratulate you on your impending marriage. That was merely to clear the way, like a sip of water before the first morsel. (*Shaking out several envelopes as Fowolu looks on, aghast*). What's four small envelopes from a servant who claims to be devoted? An insult! Where the love is genuine, the pocket is never dry. Please accept this humble contribution from me, your Lordship. Let this one be one of the most celebrated weddings of all times!

ISOLA: (*Who has been counting*). Fifteen ...sixteen ...twenty envelopes! And all filled with new notes! I'll write my report straight away! What a wonderful town! What high moral standards! Such devoted and hard-working officials! It's non-pareil! The Federal cabinet will be reshuffled without delay to include such patriotic citizens! I promise you, you'll hear from Lagos very soon. Good night.

(The Councillors bow out).

ISOLA: (*His pockets bulging*). I've got enough. Thanks, Mr Solarin! I think I can now afford to damn the rest. Yes, I'll redeem the name of the man whose reputation has made this fortune possible. Next!

(Enter the Director coughing, with a medical equipment bag).

DOCTOR: (*Coughing*). I have the honour to...to, excuse me, to present myself before you, your Excellency—Dr Bodunrin Alade-Martins...the ...the...excuse me, Chief Medical Officer in charge of the hospital.

ISOLA: (*Curtly*). What's that in your bag?

DOCTOR: It's...it's...some of the latest equipment we acquired recently. I thought you...excuse me, I thought you would like to examine them. (*Brings it forward, trembling*).

ISOLA: (*Opening it so that envelopes fall out*). What, Dr Martins? What disease are these meant to cure?

DOCTOR: (*Trembling*). You know, your...Excellency! A widespread disease...of the pocket...

ISOLA: You're in deep trouble, doctor. Trying to corrupt an official of the state.

DOCTOR: (*Coughing badly*). I...am so-r-r-rry, your Excelle-n-n...excuse me, please, they told me to... to do it. I was misled.

ISOLA: Quiet! Who misled you?

DOCTOR: The...others. They...they said...they said they all did the same thing.

ISOLA: You're lying, doctor! You want to implicate responsible and decent officials. Doctor, I am going to make sure you're properly disciplined. A man in your position should know better.

DOCTOR: But it's...it's the truth! I'll call them!!

ISOLA: Stay where you are! I hope you said a proper farewell to your wife and children tonight, for you won't be seeing them for a long time. Your new address is going to be Kirikiri.

DOCTOR: (*Crestfallen*). Kirikiri! Your Excel...Ah, in that case—

(*Before Isola can stop him, he has risen and made a desperate dash out of the room*).

ISOLA: Stop him! Arrest him! (*Runs after him, then remembers. Runs back quickly and collects envelopes. His eyes also catch the cutlass. He seizes it and runs out after the Doctor, shouting*). Stop him! He must not escape! etc.

(*Cecilia runs in, in night-gown, followed by her father*).

CECILIA: What is it? What, my darling? Are they killing you? (*The Chairman and others run in from outside*).

CHAIRMAN: Let's stay here, my friends. There's safety in numbers! I told you he's a brutal man. I, Gbonmiayelobiojo, I warned you not to provoke him! But no one listens to me, and now, blood's going to be shed! Somebody's head will fall off! There'll be *cannibality*!

PRICE CONTROL OFFICER: No, no, don't say such dreaded things. Have you no heart?

COUNCILLOR FOR COOPERATIVES: It's him! (*Pointing*). He went and dreamt up a giant rat, and since morning it's been one catastrophe after another!

PASTOR: What happened, for God's sake? Won't anyone tell me?

PRICE CONTROL OFFICER: It's your son-in-law. He's gone after Doki with a cutlass! You should see them yelling down the street.

CECILIA: I am done for! Save my husband! The Doctor will harm him.

PRICE CONTROL OFFICER: But...but your husband has the cutlass. Poor Doki is unarmed!

CECILIA: That's what I mean. The Doctor used to be an athlete. He'll outrun my poor husband to death. I'm going after them.

CHAIRMAN: No, stay my dear girl. They'll soon tire and come back. By the way, Nebu, congrats. You didn't tell me my daughter was engaged, and now I hear the wedding's tomorrow. What a way to treat a Godfather!

PASTOR: I was going to mention it, only—

BABA FAWOMI: (*Entering with Isola's diary*). Where's he? Where is the scoundrel?

PASTOR: *(Feigning indignation).* What, Baba? What are you doing in my house? Please go at once! *(Makes frantic signs at him, which are ignored).*

BABA FAWOMI: What I am doing! Listen to that! If you'd been so choosy about your visitors, you wouldn't be in the mess you're all in now, my friends.

CHAIRMAN: Can you please explain, Baba Fawomi? What *mens*?

BABA FAWOMI: Good it is you're all here. *(Looks).* Where's the Doctor?

COUNCILLOR FOR EDUCATION: Doki's busy at the moment, saving his neck from the Complaints Commissioner.

BABA FAWOMI: Quiet! That's what I mean. Which Complaints Commissioner? Didn't I tell you this morning that the Commissioner will never step in this town?

CHIEF MAGISTRATE: Yes, you did, come to think of it, but—

BABA FAWOMI: But what? I asked you to sacrifice, but did you? Answer. You did not. Instead, you brought Ifa toilet water to drink. But I forgave you, when I got home. I told myself, these people are like children, Ifa must not be angry with his children. I went and made the sacrifice, on your behalf. I'll be sending you the bill. Ifa then promised that the Commissioner will never come.

COUNCILLOR FOR EDUCATION: But he came! He's—

BABA FAWOMI: Shut up! 'But he came!' I should have expected more sense from people like you. Do you think Ifa ever breaks his word? But he came! Do you mean that a man can just walk up and say he's Solarin and you believe? What proof do you have of his identity?

PASTOR: My God, what are you saying? He has to be Solarin. He's engaged to Cecilia.

CHIEF MAGISTRATE: He has to be. He got an envelope from me.

PRICE CONTROL OFFICER: I gave him two! For his wedding.

COUNCILLOR FOR EDUCATION: Kudi gave him twenty!

COUNCILLOR FOR COOPERATIVES: He's Solarin. He's the Public Complaints Commissioner!

BABA FAWOMI: Quiet! I said, what proof do you have of his identity?

CHAIRMAN: No, no, Gbonmiayelobiojo! How can Solarin not be Solarin? My head's going in a circle!

BABA FAWOMI: Listen to this. (*He begins to read from the diary, with difficulty*) '...Dear diary, this is for your ears again ...You know how I left Lagos, shitting in my pants,'—the man is vulgar, you can see— '... fleeing from the probe and jumping bail...and I arrived in this delightful town...I walked up to the vicarage after the adventure with those robbers which I told you about. You know what happened? The Pastor's daughter fell in love with me at once—owing no doubt to my Lagos airs! And a juicy thing she is too...'

PASTOR: What! That's about my daughter?

BABA FAWOMI: It's the man's diary. Let me read on. Where am I? Yes. '...the charity of the Church must be tasted to be believed! All of a sudden, the entire town assumes I am the Public Complaints Commissioner! Can you beat that! I don't mind at all. They'll find the mistake costly. All the loot they've extracted from the poor citizens, I am going to make them vomit! (*Groans all around*). And won't I get back to Lagos in style!... Ah, I tell you they're a hilarious bunch all of them, out of the comic books!...First, there's the Chairman of the Council, Chief Gbonmi—something, a name as stupid as the man himself!'

CHAIRMAN: Impossible! That can't be there!

BABA FAWOMI: Read it yourself.

CHAIRMAN: (*Reading*). '...as stupid as the man himself.' This is a conspiracy. You wrote it!

BABA FAWOMI: Me! And where will I find all those words! I can barely read myself. This diary, I conjured up some hour ago out of the divining tray. The man you've all been crawling around is an impostor. His real name is here, Isola Oriebora

PRICE CONTROL OFFICER: Let him come back quick! I can't wait! (*Snatches the diary*). What else is in there? (*Reads*). 'The Chairman...a name as stupid as—'

CHAIRMAN: We've heard that already. No need to repeat it.

PRICE CONTROL OFFICER: There's more about you. '...I haven't met his wife yet, but Cecilia tells me she's a stark illiterate, and practically a harlot...'

CECILIA: (*Sobbing*). I never said that!

PRICE CONTROL OFFICER: (*Reading*). '...I'll try her out, with some of the poetry that disarms Cecilia...' Er...hmmmmmm...hmmmmm....

CHAIRMAN: Go on.

PRICE CONTROL OFFICER: 'The Price Control Officer is a very nice lady.'...hmmmmmm...hmmmmm...

COUNCILLOR FOR EDUCATION: What does it say? (*Snatches it and reads*). Ha! 'The Price Control Officer, from what I've seen from a distance, is a piece of stockfish...'

PRICE CONTROL OFFICER: It's his mother who's a stockfish! And his grandmother! Just let him come back here!

COUNCILLOR FOR EDUCATION: (*Reading*). 'The Councillor for Education, Chief Funso Fowolu...'—he knows my name too—'is...'Er, hmmmmm...hmmmmmm...'

PASTOR: Is what? What are you stopping for?

COUNCILLOR FOR EDUCATION: The writing's not very clear here.

COUNCILLOR FOR COOPERATIVES: (*Snatching the diary*). I'll read it, I've got good eye-sight!

COUNCILLOR FOR EDUCATION: (*Pointing*). It's easier to read further down, Kudi.

COUNCILLOR FOR COOPERATIVES: I'll read it all, my dear. Ah, there we are. '...Chief Funso Fowolu is a regular clown from what I hear. And a vicious man too, with a head shaped like a sewer, and a body odour that reminds you of the nightsoil men...'

COUNCILLOR FOR EDUCATION: Just listen to that! How imaginative can some people be?

CHIEF MAGISTRAE: (*Holding his nose and moving away*). That's true.

COUNCILLOR FOR EDUCATION: (*Reading*). '...the Chief Magistrate, I hear, is another terror...'

CHIEF MAGISTRAE: I don't know why we're reading all this rubbish. The man's not here to defend himself. In my court—

COUNCILLOR FOR COOPERATIVES: (*Reading*). '...He's a swindler and a rogue, who's enriched himself through graft, and...' Er, hmmm...hmmmm... (*Tries to shut diary*). That's all.

CHAIRMAN: (*Who has been reading over her shoulder*). Is that all indeed! Well, let me see! (*Snatches the diary*). If I, Gbomiayelobiojo, can be insulted to everyone's delight, no one is going to escape his or her turn. (*Reads*). '...The Chief Magistrate...' —no, sorry— '...The Councillor for Cooperatives is also in charge of the OFN here. An appropriate job, since she is blessed with a snout like a sow's and with legs like a hen's... The Doctor, who is an epidemic all by himself...'

PASTOR: I think this is enough.

CHAIRMAN: Wait for the last bit . '...The Pastor is a sure candidate for hell. There's still an unresolved case of missing church funds, for which I understand the Pastor wears a number of charms round his waist...'

PASTOR: And are you going to take this clown seriously?

CHAIRMAN: '...but I'm in love with the Pastor, as long as he allows me full time with his adorable daughter, Cecilia, another empty-headed fool in skirt...'

CECILIA: (*Breaks down sobbing*). You're making it all up, and you call yourself my god-father! My love's too sweet to write such things.

PRICE CONTROL OFFICER: I can't just wait till he returns. He's got another chapter coming for his diary!

(Just then the door opens. They rush at the man entering, and set upon him angrily before the screaming Polycap manages to extricate himself).

CHAIRMAN: Polycap! Ah Gbonmiayelobiojo, unlucky is the day!

POLYCAP: Master, I don die. Dis one don pass yellow fever!

(There is general embarrassment, as they all try to apologize and soothe the poor Polycap).

BABA FAWOMI: You chose an unlucky moment to come, my son. But Ifa is with you.

POLYCAP: Master, they don kill me. If I know, I for no take this message. Na the Commissioner wey send me come here

CHAIRMAN: The Commissioner! Where's he, tell me!

POLYCAP: He don go Master. He borrow your car. Madam give am the key.

CHAIRMAN: Do you hear that? The man has escaped—in my car!

BABA FAWOMI: Perhaps next time you'll learn to take Ifa seriously. This is the mark of his vengeance.

POLYCAP: (*Producing a piece of paper*). The Commissioner, he ask me to give this to Sisi. (*Gives it to Cecilia*).

CECILIA: (*Reading*) Oh no! (They *hold her from falling*).

PASTOR: What's it? Let me read it. (*Reads*). Ah, my poor child! (*They hold him from falling*).

CHAIRMAN: Give it to me. It's the task of Gbonmiayelobiojo to brave all danger on your behalf. Stand back. I'm going to read. (*Reads out*). 'My dear Cecilia, I have to leave in a hurry. The reasons you'll understand soon enough. I don't think we'll meet again. I assure you, you gave me a very good time, till you spoilt it all with the engagement by cutlass. I'll always remember you any time I take a walk along the Marina. Please, you'll find my diary somewhere in the house. Help to destroy it, it will be better that way. Goodbye, my sweet. The one who has been.'

PRICE CONTROL OFFICER: (*Crestfallen*). There is no doubt then, it's his diary!

COUNCILLOR FOR COOPERATIVES: My envelopes!
CHAIRMAN: I ask you, how could this happen to me? Ah, Gbomiayelobiojo, you've grown senile. Your brain is nothing but sawdust. Thirty years in politics, and no one could ever outsmart me! Not one Police officer could find me! Three governors, three probes, and not the slightest shred of evidence against me. And now, a simpering little punk comes up and makes a fool of me! Come, my dear people, our world is ending. We've grown old. The younger crooks have taken over the trade and they'll stop at nothing. I'm going on voluntary retirement...

(Suddenly, the song of beggars at the door. Enter Lamidi and Lemomu).

CHAIRMAN: What do you want, you two? You're fired, I hope you realize it. You started it all with your false information.
PASTOR: Who are they? What are they doing here?
LAMIDI: Lemomu shall we?
LAMOMU: We can't well refuse.
LAMIDI: It will be impolite.
LAMOMU: Official misconduct.
LAMIDI: A proof of indiscipline.
LAMOMU: Well, go ahead. After you.
LAMIDI: Excellency, we are the public's complaints—
LAMOMU: Sealed, delivered—and filed away.
LAMIDI: Sometimes we make the headlines.
LAMOMU: When we're on the side of the mighty.
LAMIDI: But often forgotten in lockers—
LAMOMU: When we back the powerless!
LAMIDI: Yes, we're words and echoes.

LAMOMU: Always clamant for justice—
LAMIDI: And always helping to postpone it.
(They go into their professional song).
CHAIRMAN: If you think you'll get a kobo out of me, you're simply dreaming. You're fired. And if you value your health you'll leave the town as fast as possible.
LAMIDI: Excellencies, there's a visitor outside.
LAMOMU: A gentleman in brown khaki shorts—
LAMIDI: And khaki shirt!
CHAIRMAN: What!
LAMOMU: The gentleman claims he's been round the town looking for the Chairman.
(Baba Fawomi slips out).
LAMIDI: The inscription on his car will surely interest you.
CHAIRMAN: Well, say it!
(The beggars start their chant again: he gives them money).
CHAIRMAN: All right, take this! What inscription?
LAMOMU: It says, 'Office of the Public Complaints Commissioner'.
ALL: What!!!
CHAIRMAN: Oh my God! Oh my head!
LAMOMU: He's here, ladies and gentlemen! He's arrived!
LAMIDI: Yes, the real Public Complaints Commissioner has arrived.

BLACKOUT. End of PLAY.

FIRST TAI SOLARIN MEMORIAL LECTURE

Delivered to the Tai Solarin Organization on July 27 2004

THE INDIVIDUAL AND THE CHALLENGES OF COMMITMENT IN AN ANOMIC SOCIETY

By
FEMI OSOFISAN

1

Lives of great men all remind us,
We can make our lives sublime
And, departing, leave behind us,
Footsteps on the sands of time.

These lines are from an English poet, Henry Wadsworth Longfellow, who lived and died in the 19th century. But, although written over a century ago, the words still speak to us with amazing pertinence, and are at the very heart of my concerns today.

But permit me, first of all, to thank the members of the Tai Solarin Organization, for the invitation to speak here this morning. I consider it an honour indeed, and a privilege, to have been selected to give the very first Annual Memorial Lecture in remembrance of the life of such a remarkable man.

As most of you know, I myself am not an *ex-May*, as you the alumni of the Mayflower College, Ikenne, are called. But all my years of adolescence, all my teenage years, were filled with the clamour of the exploits of Tai Solarin in the cause of social justice, and I grew up to young adulthood in intense admiration of him.

That was why, in 1978, I wrote my play, *Who's Afraid of Solarin?*, both to celebrate and immortalize his name, and also call attention to the gross corruption that was rampant in public life at the time. One of my proudest moments therefore has been that evening at the famous Arts Theatre of the university of Ibadan, when Tai—that was how he insisted on being addressed by young and old—sat by my side to watch the world première of the play. Our conversation afterwards in his hotel room on Ring Road has also remained as a permanent memento in my diary of cherished encounters.

Official corruption was of course—you all remember—one of the ills that Tai fought passionately against, and on that front, perhaps the most memorable opportunity for him to actually lead a war against it came in 1976, when he was offered the post of Public Complaints Commissioner, a kind of official Ombudsman, for the whole of the then Western State of Nigeria.

You will recall that Tai was not the only one to be so appointed. Similar appointments were made for other states in the Federation. But who remembers now the names of the other appointees or one single action that they took? Yet even when the precise details have faded from memory, Tai's fiery battles in the assignment remain in our minds, like items of immemorial myth.

Solarin's colleagues had apparently chosen to play the game that the government intended for them—that is, to act as mere smokescreen for reform, and put up a charade of empty threats and harmless gesticulations, while business continued as usual in government circles.

They were to pretend to be investigating corruption, with appropriate noise and bombast like true mountebanks, and through such antics, help deceive the people that responsible action was being taken in answer to their complaints, and also assure them that culprits would be brought to book. That way, the rising anger of the public would be attenuated and the growing number of critics lulled into silence.

It was Solarin alone who refused to play his role according to that immoral government script. He took the business of his assignment seriously, as a long-awaited challenge at last to purge the society and the government bureaucracy of its pests. He became an avid hunter of the rogues in power. In the full glare of the public, he exposed the cupidity of those supposed to be serving us, but who were busy stuffing their own pockets instead.

This was a totally unprecedented procedure by someone supposed to be a government official! Tai was sowing panic everywhere, while an incredulous public cheered him on with uproarious delight!

Naturally then he could not have lasted long in the post— and he didn't! As we say in Yoruba, *'igi gongonron má gún mi l'ójú, òkèèrè la tí nyèé nù!...'* When those who appointed him discovered, with great embarrassment that they could not cage nor control him, they became frightened, reading correctly in his campaign a threat that the loose cannon they themselves had unwittingly unleashed would explode on them too sooner or later, if they did not act quickly to pre-empt him! Abruptly therefore they relieved him of the post, making him submit a dubious letter of resignation over a trivial affair.

Thus ended what could have been an established tradition of public probity in our history.

2

I took great interest in this story of course at the time, as a Tai votarist. But what impressed me even more was its aftermath. What did the rest of the people do, in response to Solarin's dismissal?

There was, to be sure, an immediate upwelling of protesting voices at the beginning. But just as quickly as they rose, these voices also rapidly faded out. A number of letters were published immediately after the incident, lauding Solarin's courage and outstanding zeal, and his achievements in office. Many hailed him as a hero, just as they had done on a number of occasions before. Many even went as far as castigating the government for its undisguised duplicity. But in a month or so, all was over. Quietly we all dropped back into our habitual muteness.

No one stood up to organize a march against the government action. There were no public demonstrations insisting that the man be reinstated, or demanding that the unfinished cases he exposed be pursued to their logical conclusion, in open prosecution. Most of us had simply resigned ourselves to letting things remain as they were.
I was, and am still fascinated, because I was noticing for the first time this phenomenon which seems to define the fixed pattern of our social and political behaviour—namely, an eager volition always to surrender and to let sleeping dogs lie, as opposed to standing and confronting crisis.

This has been our customary response to the repeated mauling, by the state and its agents, of those we ourselves have enthusiastically hailed as our heroes. Practically all the people we have worshipped and promoted as ideal models in the tumultuous adventure of our country since Independence have ended up being brutalized, chased to exile, or even exterminated by the forces of the state, with only the rare instance of vocal protest on our part.

We laud their audacious interventions of course, but hardly do we strive to emulate them. We admire their acts of valour, but we seem to be so cowed by the enormous costs they are made to pay, that we would not ourselves dare to deviate from the mundane course of complacency and timid acceptance that we have mapped out for our lives.

This is the grand paradox I want us to explore today. Our solidarity is always spontaneous and genuine for these outspoken rebellious figures, of this there is no doubt. Our admiration of them is equally sincere, filled with the appropriate reverence. But it is an adulation without teeth; without even the desire to bite.

To judge from the examples of Awojobi, Fela Ransome-Kuti, Kudirat Abiola, and—how many others?—the only time, it seems, that we are able to speak openly and acknowledge our heroes, is when they have been turned into corpses and we write their obituaries.

So the question that Solarin's experience raised for me then, which I have not yet been able to resolve, and which I will now pose to you who had more intimate relationship with the man is this—is our society not in fact too comfortable with evil, too content let corruption thrive as long as its perpetrators do not disturb our 'peace', to be worthy of any individual sacrifice? If the role we have assigned to the individual conscience in our midst is no different from that of a fatuous martyrdom, is radicalism then not a waste, a merely quixotic gesture, the fruit of a futile and deluded idealism?

And so, is the kind of memorial we are holding today not a disguised mockery of the dead, or merely a ceremonial rite of appeasement, to purge our conscience of collective guilt? In other words, did Solarin die in vain?

3

Before you answer, however, permit me to complicate these questions a bit further. Today, it is ten years now since Solarin left us and, in those ten years, things seem to have grown considerably worse. Worse for all of us, and not only the common man.

We used to say, when the soldiers were here, that we lived in a season of *locusts*. Nowadays, with the civilians in power, the common consensus on the street is that we have entered the Age of *Leeches*—that is, of locusts in a new garb.

Civilian rule, as far as the majority of our people are concerned, has merely proved to be like the NYSC, which is mockingly translated as *Now Your Suffering Continues*.

Democracy has come, but if you ask most people, they will tell you that it is still a long wait yet, even after five years, for its dividends. Of course we did not expect things to change overnight or without pain. But five years cannot be called 'overnight', nor can people be faulted if they grow despondent at the persistent lack of improvement in their lives. Even the few positive gains that one can point at come with one comma or other.

Thus, unlike before, we are all free, for instance, to talk now as we wish to our leaders; but so are they equally free to shut their ears, and not to hear our complaints.

In the same vein, modern communications and air travel have improved tremendously, but they function erratically, and at costs much heavier than the average purse can bear.

Hunger still rules the streets. Violence and danger are rampant. Life is cheap. Under the double menace of armed robbers and armed security personnel in various uniforms, every one has learnt the wisdom of treading with care even in the daylight.

In the cities, urban squalor is a monster we are still unable to tame; in the villages, poverty has driven the youths away from the farms. In spite of the President's fervent campaign, corruption is still rife, especially at the state and local government levels, such that the play I wrote for Solarin in 1978 to castigate official sleaze is still today as tragically pungent and pertinent.

Insecurity, poverty and unemployment, these have become the indomitable problems of our time. And their impact is further aggravated by the frequent lack of compassion at the highest levels of governance. So it is not a nation we have, say some people; but rather, a state of anomy.

In reaction against this dismal situation of our country, many of us, I said above, have chosen the option of silence, or outright complicity, in order to get on with their lives. But in the ten years of Solarin's death, owing largely to economic and political developments on the international scene, a third option has come to offer itself readily to the beleaguered Nigerian—and this is the option of emigration. It is the option that has become the most popular with our youths especially.

Practically every young man you meet nowadays has decided to flee to other lands; practically every woman is frantically seeking a way of escape abroad. Out of every four in any family, three are convinced that Nigeria is a lost adventure, that hope is not where the home is, but outside, across the boarder.

Hence the visa lines grow longer daily at the foreign embassies, especially of the USA, the European countries, and even China and South Africa. Correspondingly the stories of deliberate cruelty, of horrendous abasement, meted out to these asylum seekers, both on departure and arrival, multiply on the daily headlines.

But yet, the passion to emigrate does not abate. If anything, the humiliation only seems to increase the desperation.

Are these then the three available options to us today to cope with our situation of pain and anomy? Do we have no choices, in our legitimate pursuit of happiness for ourselves and our families, other than complicity, apathy, or escape; than compromise, or collaboration, or emigration?

I mean, is it true that the sane Nigerian, who does not want to die of frustration, must either procure a ticket and a visa, and run away across the border; or if he stays, he must meekly agree to join the game—pay the bribe without complaint when asked, make his own loot quietly when chanced, ask no questions of the thieving leader but eagerly join his fawning train instead, turn wilfully blind to whatever cruelty or agony that may be going on around him, and never speak out in defence of truth?

What precisely should be the role of the individual in a failed state like ours?

But I am not going to ask you to answer these questions yet. Most of you, I presume, must have made your decisions long ago. Some of you have undoubtedly sent your children abroad already, far from our 'madding crowd', or are preparing to do so, convinced that our country is a case beyond redemption.

Some others, unwilling or perhaps unable to get away, have resigned themselves abjectly to fate, to the sorry conclusion that they are trapped here, like animals in a zoo run by lunatics, and that their best means of survival is by tame and unquestioning compliance with the instructions of the zookeeper. So when the government shouts 'Jump!', their hasty answer is, 'How high, sir?'

What, I wonder, would Solarin have had to say to all this?

4

The first title I suggested for this lecture, when I was contacted was '*Gbokugboku*: the Individual as the Communal Undertaker and Scapegoat.' Then frantic calls came from the organizers. '*Gbokugboku*', for those who do not speak Yoruba literally means 'the carrier of corpses'. Corpses! The organizers were, perhaps justly, apprehensive that to announce a title with such a morbid word might scare away some of their potential audience. Some people are very sensitive about such things! And I wonder in fact how many of you here today would have come if I had insisted on keeping the title?

Anyway I agreed to change it to something more agreeable. But as I proceed, you will see that its essence is still very much the kernel of my speech today. For, although '*Gbokugboku*' does translate indeed as 'the carrier of corpses', it is only disturbing when taken in its literal sense. It has a metaphorical dimension however, a connotation more profound than the surface meaning, in which it assumes positive significance.

The reason why I have been drawn to use it is in fact quite simple, and not because I have any perverse fascination for corpses. As some of you will remember, the word was one of the nicknames which some of our compatriots perversely gave to Tai when he was alive.

The nickname was invented deliberately to deride the man. It was meant to mock him and discourage him from one of the civic duties that Tai had chosen to perform, against the prevailing common tide. For Tai Solarin was never one to see a corpse on the road and simply pass by, as the rest of us would do. That was how the name came about.

At that time, just as nowadays, one of the recurrent scandals in our nation was the sight of dead bodies dumped regularly on the highway, and which would remain there for weeks unclaimed, till they rotted away. Invariably these bodies would carry various signs of deliberate mutilation—with perhaps the head, or a limb, or the private organs, shaved off.

But it was not just this gruesome sight, as unsettling as it was, that was the scandal; nor even the shocking contemplation that some of our countrymen could be so desperate and so ruthless as to assault their fellow men in this crude and barbarous manner,.

The real scandal, as far as Tai saw it, was in the way we reacted, we who saw these corpses. Of course, our first reaction would be the expected shock and revulsion. We would exclaim and shake our head and click our tongues with the appropriate hisses and cries of alarm. But almost immediately afterwards, we would turn our eyes aside, and hurry away, probably muttering prayers and invoking the blood of Jesus!

But that's all we would do. None of us would take any step about having the corpse removed, not to talk of giving it an appropriate decent burial. The body would therefore lie there untouched, and begin slowly to bloat and decompose before our very eyes.

Day after day we would pass by and watch this gory drama, shaking our heads at the spectacle of a once-human body disintegrating slowly, its flesh gradually drying and peeling off the bones, till the rest of the carcass was cleaned off by weather and vermin. Or sometimes, particularly in the busy streets of the large towns, it is vehicles that would run over the corpses, scatter them into fragments on the tar, and carry the bits away, plastered to the tyres.

After the first day, as we continued to pass by in our helplessness, we would gradually lose our shock and outrage, and reconcile ourselves to the view. The dead body would become just another debris on the road, just another abandoned piece of refuse.

And in the course of time, petty traders or food vendors would be seen calmly erecting their counters and carrying on their trade with bubbling enthusiasm right next to some decomposing human corpse!

And even churches, or mosques, would be conducting their services enthusiastically, with some corpse rotting away just outside one of the windows!

That was the picture in Tai Solarin's time; and it is still, very sadly, the same scenario today. Mysteriously mutilated corpses are still being dumped on our highways. They lie there and decompose there, while we walk by and turn our eyes somewhere else.

But—No!, Tai said one day. No humane society should be allowed to continue to treat its citizens this way. Death should not be an excuse for the ill-treatment of the dead, even if we were uncertain about the corpse's identity! We could not continue to neglect the obligation of decency we owe one another as human beings, whether dead or alive.

So, whenever he saw another body on the road, Solarin would interrupt his journey, go and purchase a coffin, seek some helping hands, and carry the corpse to the nearest police station. Again and again he did this, dragging journalists along, trying to goad the police into action, and get them to do their duty, with the power of public embarrassment.

It was a singularly compassionate, and courageous, undertaking. Solarin was teaching us a necessary lesson, the rest of us, that there is a solidarity between all human beings which no circumstances should or can erase.

Above all, he was also showing us, by direct personal involvement, that neither indifference nor evasion is a choice in any matter that concerns another human being or contributes to the public good.

5

I have chosen this episode advisedly, to illustrate one man's concrete response to the questions I raised above.

The problems facing our country are myriad all right, but they are not insurmountable, to judge from the history of other countries, especially those we consider a paradise today. Our problems are no different from those that other countries faced before us and defeated.

For no country ever gets better unless its citizens are prepared to first undertake the necessary struggle, and make the requisite sacrifice, that it would take to make it so.

The attractive situation of these other countries we admire today would not have existed if their citizens had chosen to run away, and had not committed themselves, at the crucial moments, to confronting their own crises of social, economic, and political development. If their grandfathers had preferred to be merely placid and compliant, their children would have had no cause to be so arrogantly comfortable today!

This is the harsh truth that Solarin's example so vividly illustrates, that with courage and compassion, we can change many things in our lives. Unfortunately we do not listen or follow him, because we have allowed ourselves to be immobilized by fear.

When we hasten away, as we do, from these abandoned bodies, we know we do so, not because we are incapable of pity or compassion, nor because we are not aware that it is wrong to behave like this towards the remains of a fellow human being. When we turn our heads and quicken our steps to get away, it is not that we do not experience some twinge of guilt, however minimal, at our own display of callousness.

We do so because of one thing—our fear!

We know we could go to the police to report the matter, and have the corpse removed. But we also know that, in such matters, the police is not always our friend. More likely than not, your attempt to be a good Samaritan would end up with the police holding you as the first suspect, as a culprit or an accomplice trying to cover up your tracks! And the least consequence of your daring, of your interference, would be several wasted hours at the police station, if you didn't end up in the dock in fact, defending yourself against a charge of murder!

So, because of this, we take care not to get involved, and hope that the police would eventually arrive on their own to pick up the corpse. Unfortunately however, they never do, and we know it. Indeed, patrol cars are often among the vehicles driving recklessly over the broken corpses! But none among us would dare approach them to get them to do their civic duty. Timidly we kill our conscience, and return to our own preoccupations.

And there is still an additional fear. How for instance—we would ask ourselves—was one to be sure, if one got involved, that one would not inadvertently make oneself a target of the occult forces for which the unknown victim was sacrificed? This kind of fear may sound irrational now in this assembly, but we know that it is in fact the more powerful disincentive against our natural reflex to do something about these abandoned bodies. For there is almost none of us, whether Christian or Muslim, who is immune to this fear of occult forces, and hence of inadvertently inviting some curse upon his head.

So how can we forget that, once upon a time, one man among us discovered that he could no longer live and continue to pass by these corpses and still remain at peace with himself? He realized that, whenever he went past like that, turning away his eyes, he felt something vital give within himself, something he could not describe, an inner wrench like the loss of his soul. He felt somehow diminished each time, to the extent that shame completely overwhelmed him. And he felt then that he could no longer be indifferent.

Greater then than this man's terror of the police, of the possibility of their bringing complications into his daily routine, and greater than any fear of getting into collision with some awesome cult, was this fear he could not silence, of losing respect for himself and severing his bonds with humanity.

That man was Tai Solarin.

He told himself that it is our duty, as fellow human beings, to ensure a decent burial for the dead; that it is a duty that we owe, not so much to the dead in fact, but to ourselves as human beings.

Thus, if anyone turned away from such a duty, out of cowardice, then such a man did not deserve the name; did not deserve to live!

Solarin was able to remind himself of all this only because of the qualities he possessed, of a deep compassion, and personal courage. When he embarked on his lonely campaign to clear the streets of these stray corpses, he was rescuing the rest of us from our shameful pusillanimity.

6

The significant thing however about this issue of abandoned corpses is that it was not an isolated act, but in fact quite characteristic of Solarin's ebullient life. It was certainly one of the most startling instances of his dogged commitment to the communal well-being, but there were several others.

And because of this, paradoxically—(but perhaps not surprisingly in the end)—he aroused passionate reactions. Because his actions sprang, as they only could, from a man of strong convictions and uncommon courage, that was bound to irritate and enrage those that were cowardly and cynical—which is to say, the majority of us.

Because Tai demonstrated unusual selflessness and benignancy, his example was bound to provoke the normally callous and self-centred; it was bound to unmask the sanctimonious posturing of our teeming population of religious devotees, who would never take such actions themselves in spite of their professed zealotry.

Solarin was attracting bitter envy from some of his contemporaries therefore, who did not have the courage to do what he was doing, and instead of admiration and tumultuous applause, he was winning enemies and acrimonious criticism. These antagonists were the ones who sought to bring him down in public esteem by all sorts of strategies, including persecution and derisive abuse. They were the ones who finally thought up a nickname they thought would denigrate him: '*Gbokugboku*', the carrier of corpses, the busybody who had nothing else to do than take up the job of undertakers!

But this did not however deter the man. Solarin was not the kind of man to run away from a tough situation. He had created for himself the role of society's self-appointed conscience, a scapegoat willing to risk his life on behalf of the common good. And he knew that no scapegoat ever escapes the crown of thorns.

Solarin was a man of steel, and where principle was concerned, he could not be bent.

He knew that posterity is what matters, more than the blind and transient judgment of contemporaries; that death is like a distillation process, in which the true worth of any individual finally receives its polish, and the man of honour attains his apotheosis.

That is why it is our name that lives after us, and why, many years after his death, we are gathered here to celebrate Tai Solarin, just as he will continue to be remembered, even years after we ourselves would have gone to join him.

So it is Tai who is having the last laugh today! Instead of humiliating him as they intended to do, his enemies were in fact conferring on him a badge of respect! For the name

'*Gbokugboku*' is a title which, in my opinion, Solarin and his family should be proud of.

Yes, Solarin took care of corpses, but in a sense that was far beyond the narrow, prosaic manner that his detractors imagined. He was '*Gbokugboku*' in that larger metaphorical sense of a visionary undertaker seeking to restore light and sanity to our sick society.

Just as he fought to have dead bodies cleared from our streets, so Tai fought, and just as fiercely too, to clear away the hundreds of dead ideas that litter and suffocate our minds, and bury the decayed habits that continue to clutter our culture.

Solarin found our society pullulating with the foul remains of decadent customs and corrupted practices, and he set himself the task, even against the complicit indifference or the corroding opposition of his contemporaries, to clean up the mess and make the society sane again.

He showed us that too many corpses have been dumped along the streets of our lives, which continue to bring impediments to our development. And the most pernicious and the most pervasive among them, in his view, were the corpses of tradition and orthodoxy; the cadavres of religiosity and fatalism; and the open sores of complacency.

Solarin lived all his life, striving to clear all these corpses away, especially from the road travelled by the young.

He was particularly interested in the young, in the budding generation. He directed his newspaper columns mainly at them, giving counsel, denouncing indolence and corruption, affirming hope in their future. 'May your road be rough!' he prayed at one point, insisting that adversity was the only route to wisdom and wealth. And at another moment, he warned that 'No ambitious and courageous young man should look before he leaps... because the big fish is never caught in shallow waters.' By this he meant that the only future anybody can expect, is the one we work hard to create for ourself.

Solarin took the area of education as a virtual battlefield for the preparation of the leaders of tomorrow, and he started a school for them where he taught the habits of diligence, self-reliance, dedication and independence. You are all the proud products today of the man's prodigious vision.

7

I want to cite one more instance, and then I am done. One of the areas where the dead habits of tradition show most clearly is in our love of superficiality and of appearances, particularly in our habits of dressing, where we tend to take the robe for the monk.

Gleefully we associate finery and expensive clothes with nobility, dignity and probity, to the extent that charlatans find it easy to take advantage of this weakness to get the better of us. Invariably therefore nowadays, the crooks and fraudsters are the most elaborately and elegantly turned out. Embroidered gowns and costly beads and jewellery adorn clever tricksters and callous gangsters. The '419ers' wear glittering adornments and are spontaneously accorded precedence wherever they go. Fashion becomes the ready mask for criminality. Debauchery struts triumphantly in the disguise of damask.

Solarin tried his hardest, while he was with us, to unveil this hypocrisy by the best means he knew—which was by the precept of his personal life. In a manner that many considered idiosyncratic, but which he presented as a symbolic model, Solarin chose to fill his wardrobe with nothing more than a khaki short and khaki shirt, plus an emblematic khaki cap. This was what—except during that one notorious moment of temptation—he wore throughout his career as a social activist, trying to demonstrate that it is the human being that matters, and not what he uses to embellish himself.

8

One can continue with more telling instances of Tai's non-conformity, prescribed by an extraordinary spirit of concern for others, especially the young. But I believe I have spoken enough now for you to be able to formulate a clear answer to the questions I posed above.

Tai would never, like us, have even thought of the option of running away from our midst, however desperate things may be. Nor would he have accepted the other choice of watching meekly as things deteriorate.

Especially on behalf of the poor, who seem nowadays to have lost the war of survival to the priests of market forces, Solarin would have risen as spokesman and noisy defender. But he would have had little pity, it is certain, for the asylum seekers or the youths wandering the streets of the cities in search of white collar jobs or in suicidal pursuit of crime.

For Tai, each person's fate is literally in his hands, in his ability and willingness to create wealth for himself by his own labour and sweat. If we accept that as a fundamental principle, then it follows that, if we put our minds and our shoulders to it, we can make our society what we want it to be, all of us working together towards that single goal. ·

A very old man was seen one day, working in the small garden in front of his house. And as he worked, grunting and sweating, he would pause and sing cheerfully:

I'm weeding and planting
And sweating and panting

Chorus:
Seeds, oh seeds!
Please grow well,
And bear fruits for me!

Though tired and tender
I won't surrender

Chorus:
Seeds, oh seeds, etc...

A man passing by saw the old man at work, the way he applied himself so assiduously, and stopped to watch in wonder. But the old man went on with his work, cutting and hacking away, completely oblivious to his presence.

Then a second person, a young woman hawking *wosiwosi*, also came along, and could not but stop also to watch. Then another person also stopped. And another, till a crowd had gathered, all pointing and laughing.

But the old man worked on, as if he did not see them, and now and then, as before, would pause to sing:

I'm weeding and planting
And sweating and panting

Chorus:
Seeds, oh seeds!

Please grow well,
And bear fruits for me!

Though tired and tender
I won't surrender

Chorus:
Seeds, oh seeds, etc...

At last one of the on-lookers stepped forward and stopped the old man. 'Old man,' he said, barely holding his laughter, 'what are you working yourself so hard for, planting these fruit trees? How long do you think it will take them to mature and bear fruit, and how much longer do you expect to live?'

'Ah, that's the point!" replied the old man. 'I expect to die soon, so these trees I'm planting are not for me, but for those who will be coming after me. I want them to eat the fruits, just as I ate from the labour of those who came before me!'

And with that, he turned away to continue his work, singing:
I'm weeding and planting
And sweating and panting

Chorus:
Seeds, oh seeds!
Please grow well,
And bear fruits for me!

Though tired and tender
I won't surrender

Chorus:
Seeds, oh seeds, etc...

This is the message I have for you this morning, a message that Solarin's life so aptly illustrated. Let us do the weeding and planting today, so our children will not only reap the harvest of our labour, but will also learn from us the habit of planting for tomorrow.

For nobody anywhere will change the society for us, except we ourselves. But there should be no despair, because already the Creator has endowed us with all the tools we require, namely, intelligence and wit, courage and compassion—a capacity for laughter and companionship, a boundless imagination and a brain to think with, a heart to feel, hands to work, and feet to put our imprints down on the sands of time. Tai possessed all these qualities in abundance, and was always ready to invest them in the quest for the communal good.

This is what makes his anniversary significant, because it allows us to remember one of the heroes who never deserted us, but who, in spite of vilification and persecution, lived every one of his moments by a doctrine of intrepid and unflinching commitment.

Lives of great men—said the poet—*all remind us,*
We can make our lives sublime
And, departing, leave behind us,
Footsteps on the sands of time.

Footsteps that, perhaps another,
Sailing o'er life's solemn main,
A forlorn and shipwreck'ed brother,
Seeing, shall take heart again.

Let us then be up and doing,
With a heart for any fate;
Still achieving, still pursuing,
Learn to labour and to wait.

These words could have been a chapter in Tai Solarin's writings. 'Let us then be up and doing'! How many times, and through how many acts of valour, Tai echoed these same exhortations!

He taught us, by his exemplary life, that the individual has a value in society, and that this value increases in proportion to our involvement in the struggle for our mutual happiness.

Once again, I thank you for the honour of inviting me.

Femi Osofisan.
July 2004.

www.ingramcontent.com/pod-product-compliance
Lightning Source LLC
Chambersburg PA
CBHW011746220426
43667CB00019B/2920